Grab you coloring books, Grab your
pencils Let's Color

None of our artwork is computer generated. All is original free hand artwork. Call and ask about our specialty , custom artwork, minimum order 20 books. Have a book custom designed for your childs birthday, Include his/her picture on the cover. We Can create a coloring book as a fund raiser for your project. Theswe books are being ordered for advertising of businesses, birthday any age, weddings, . . . You decide.

256-201-7584

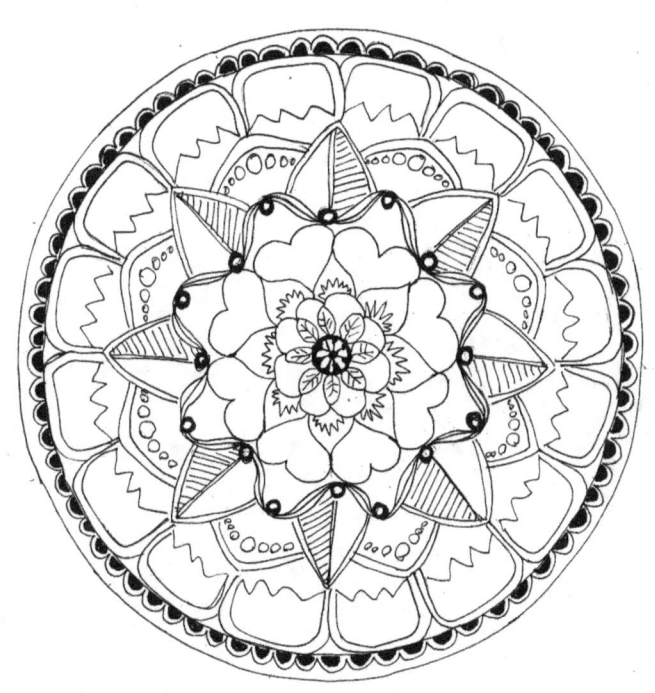

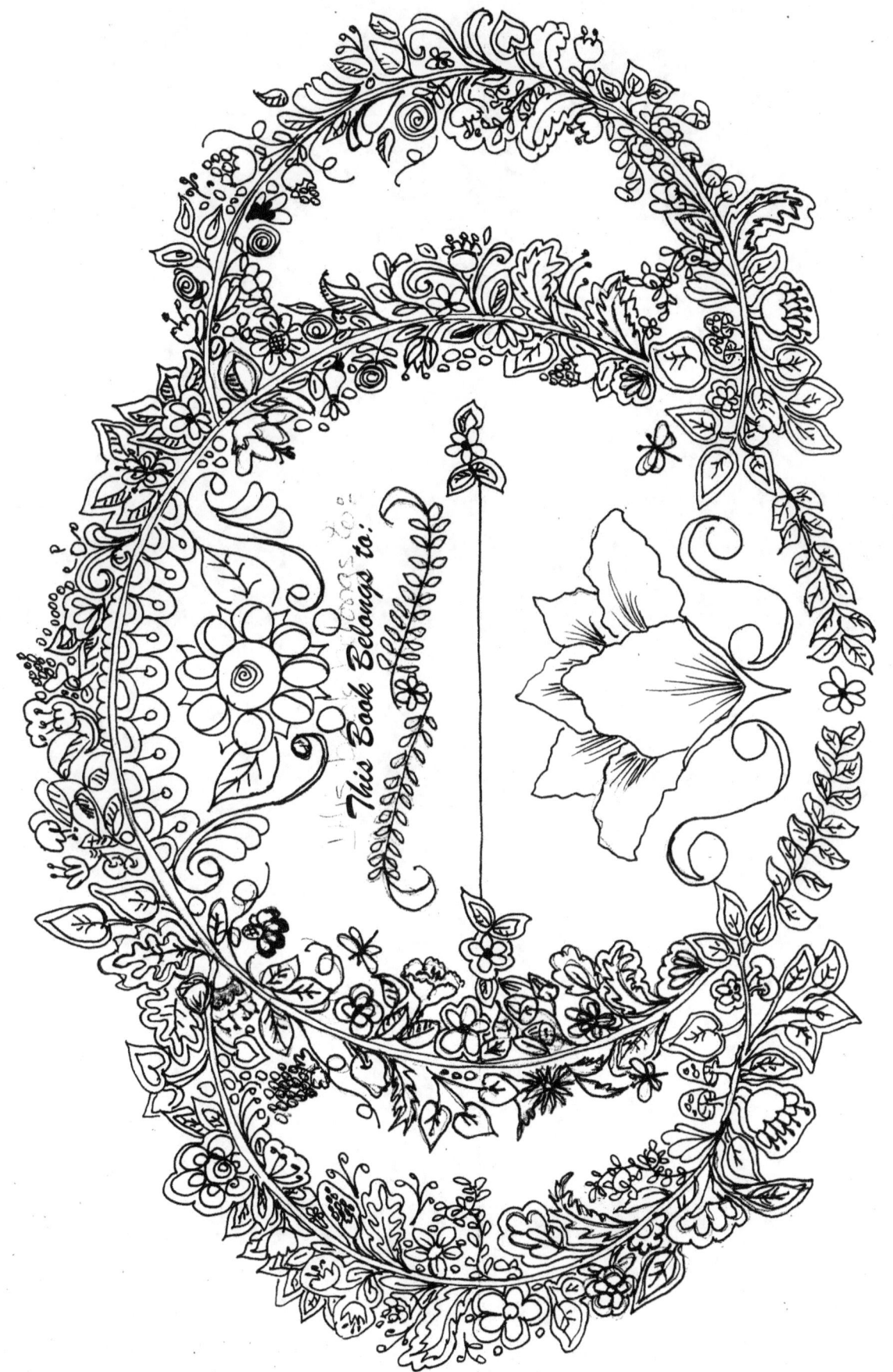

This Book Belongs to:

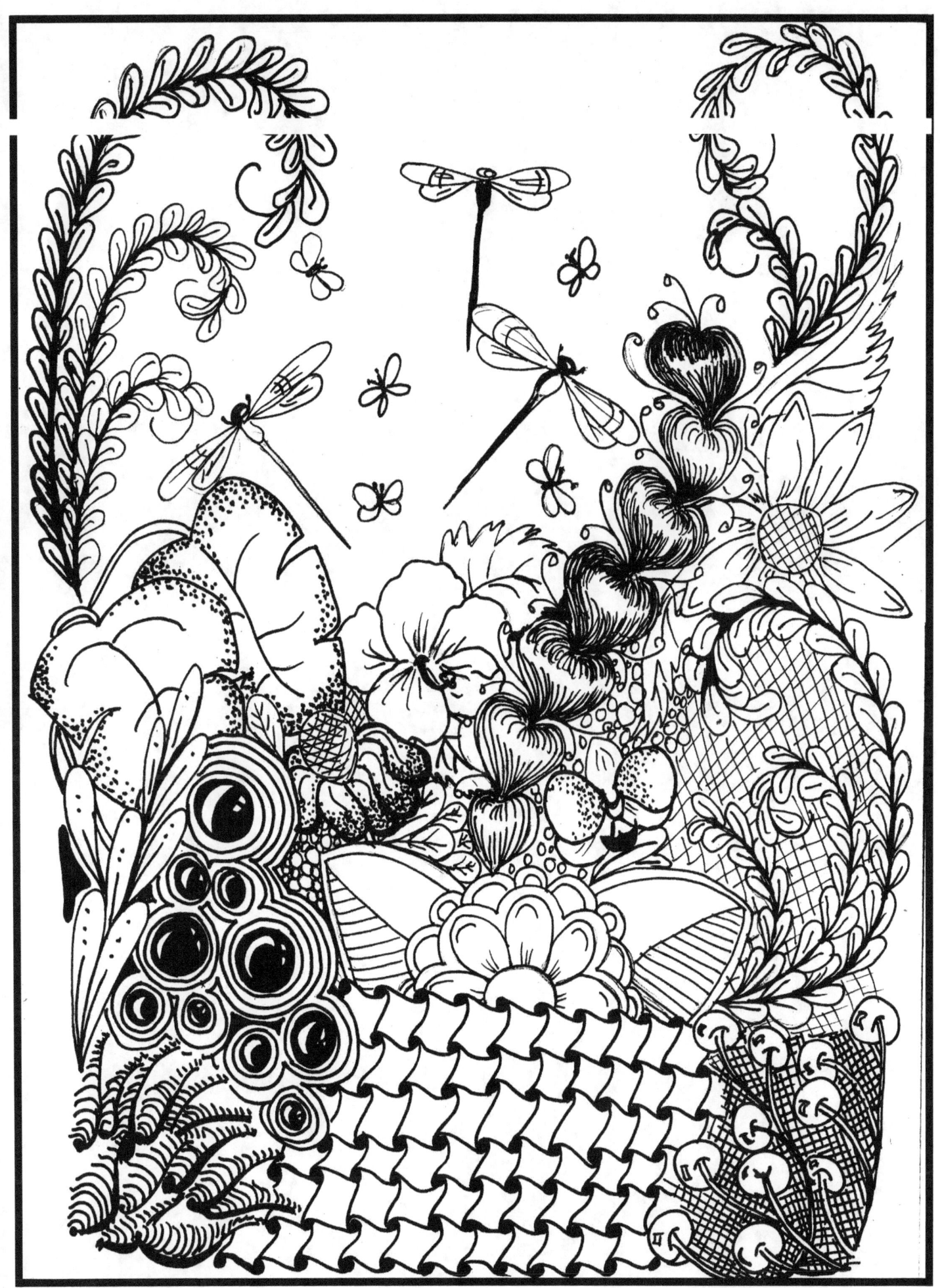

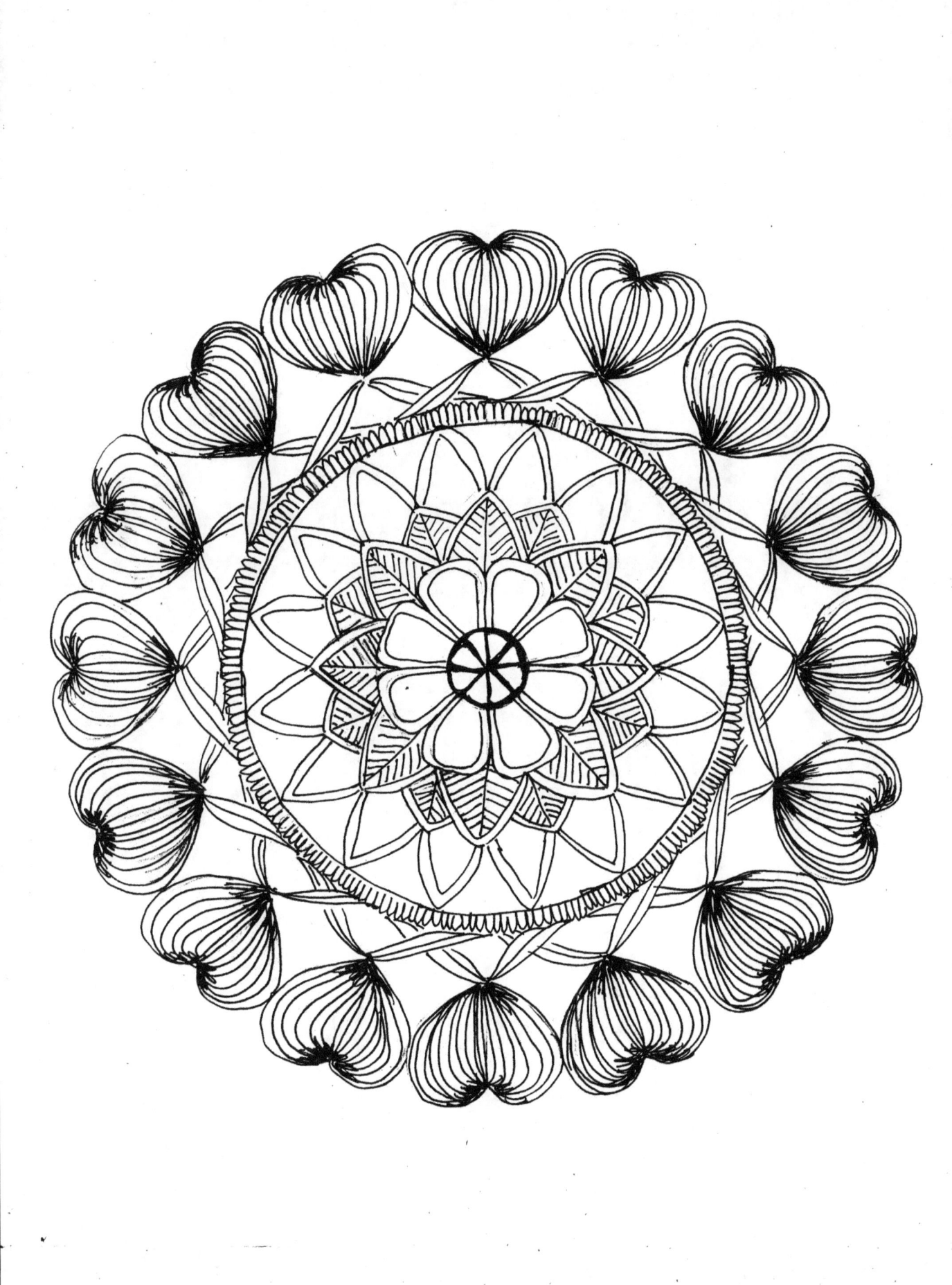

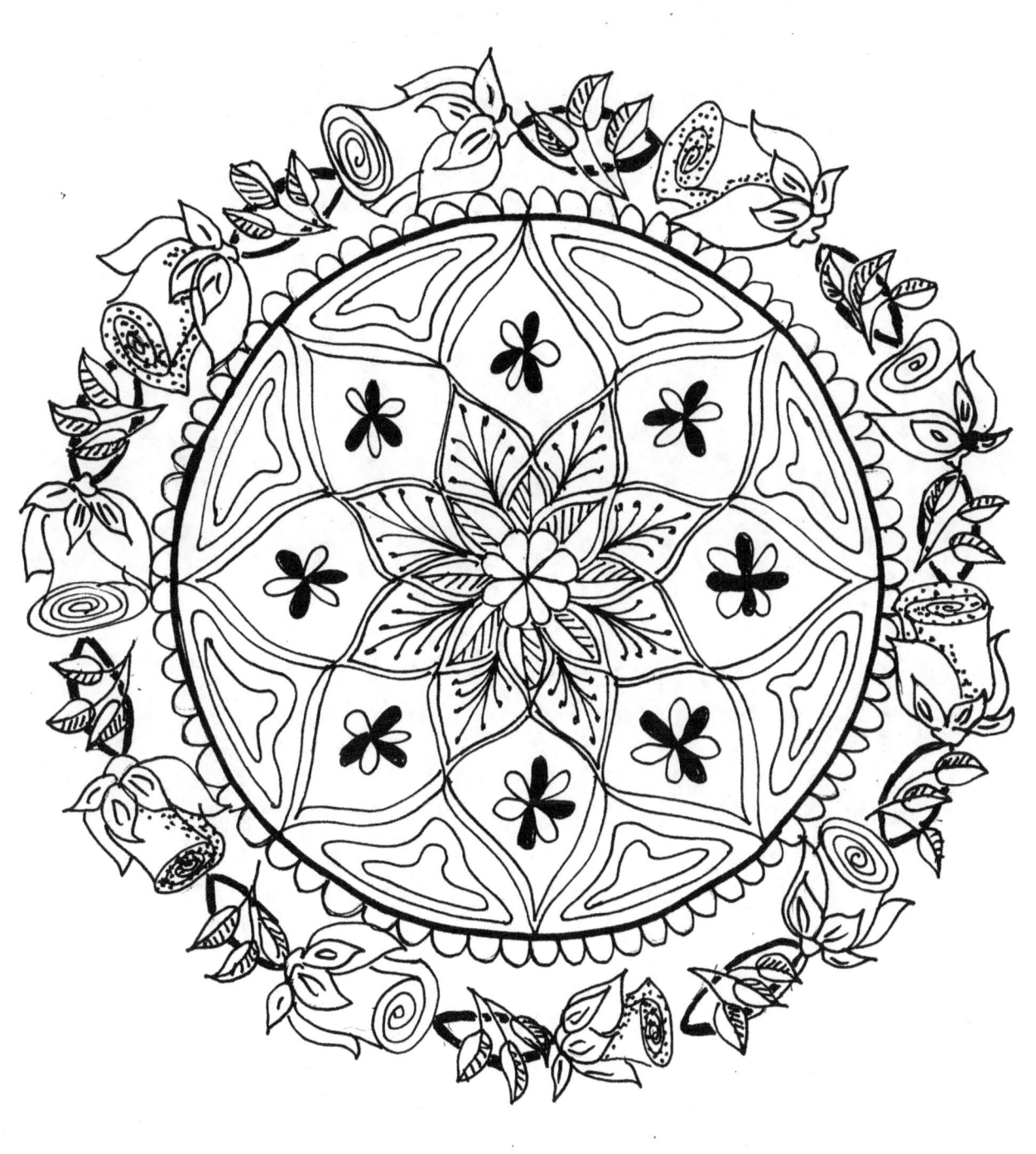

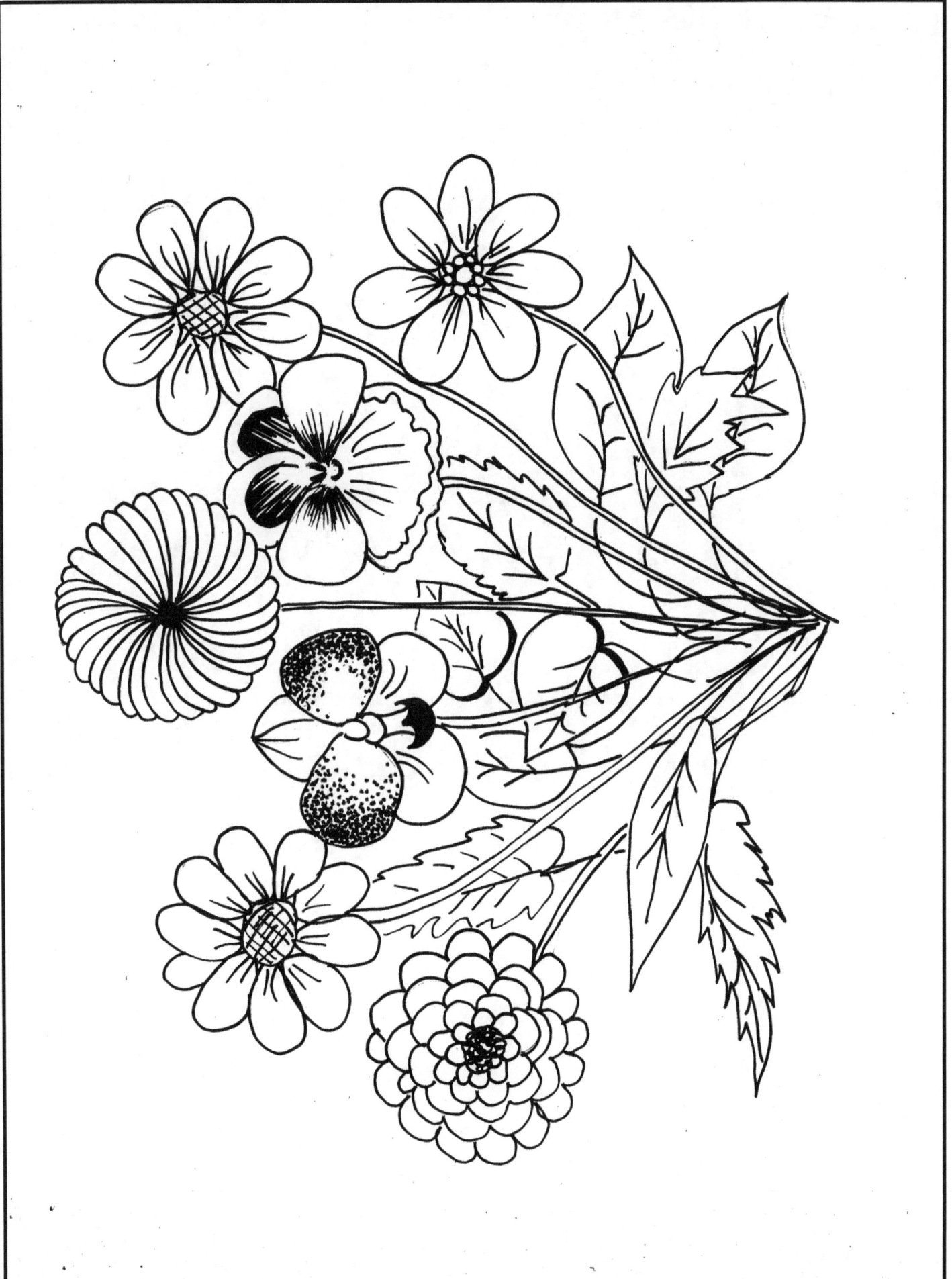

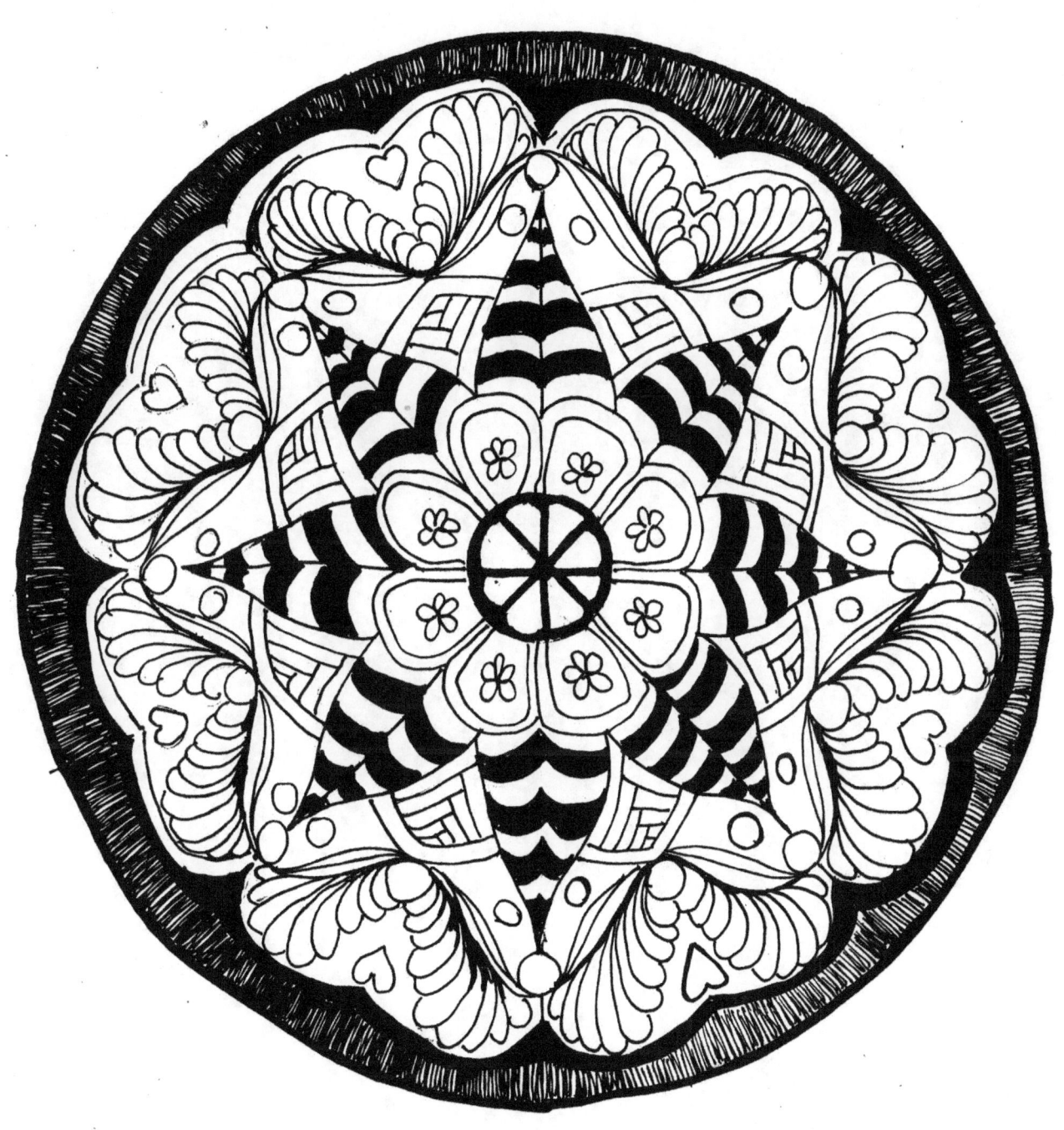

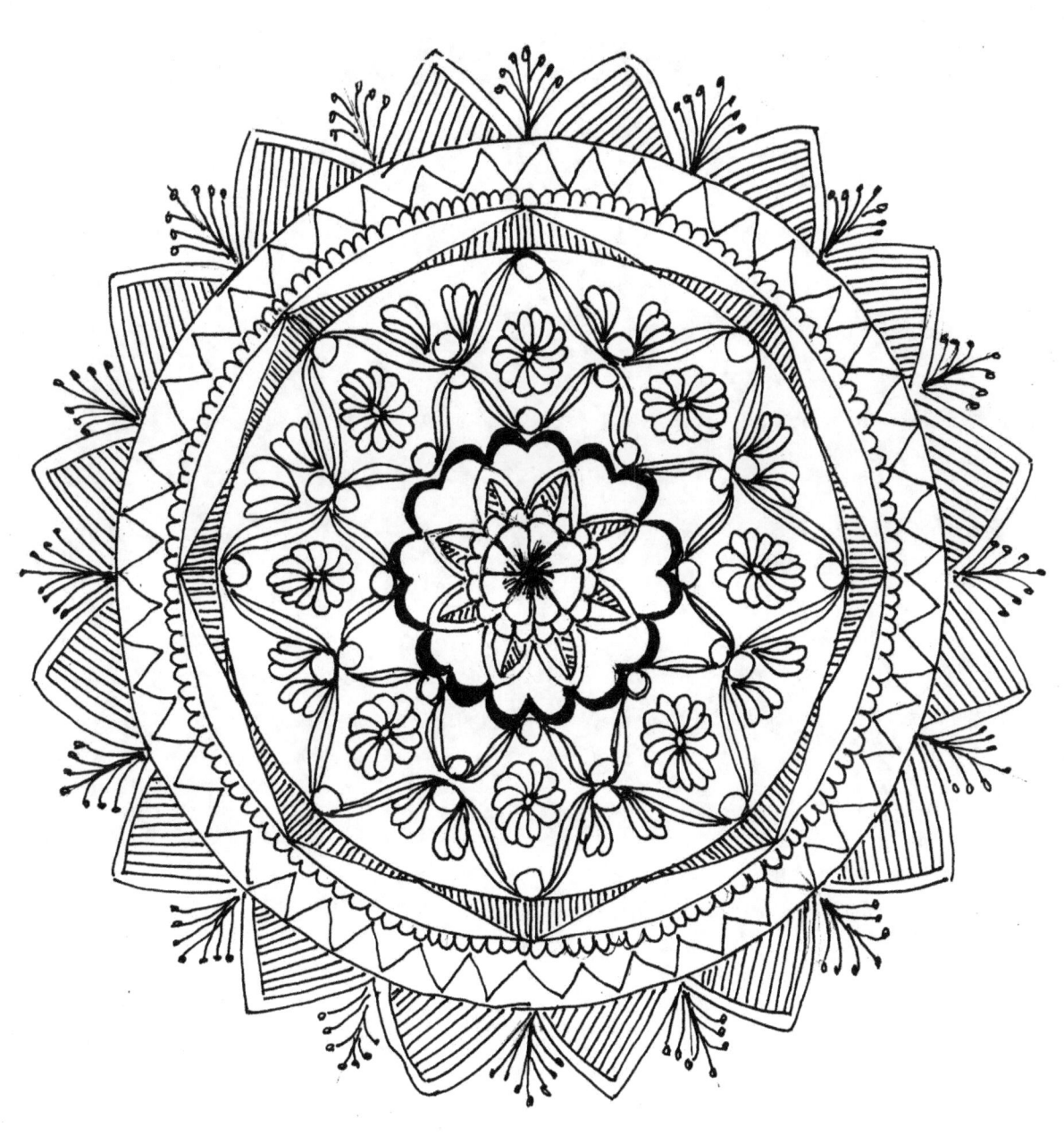

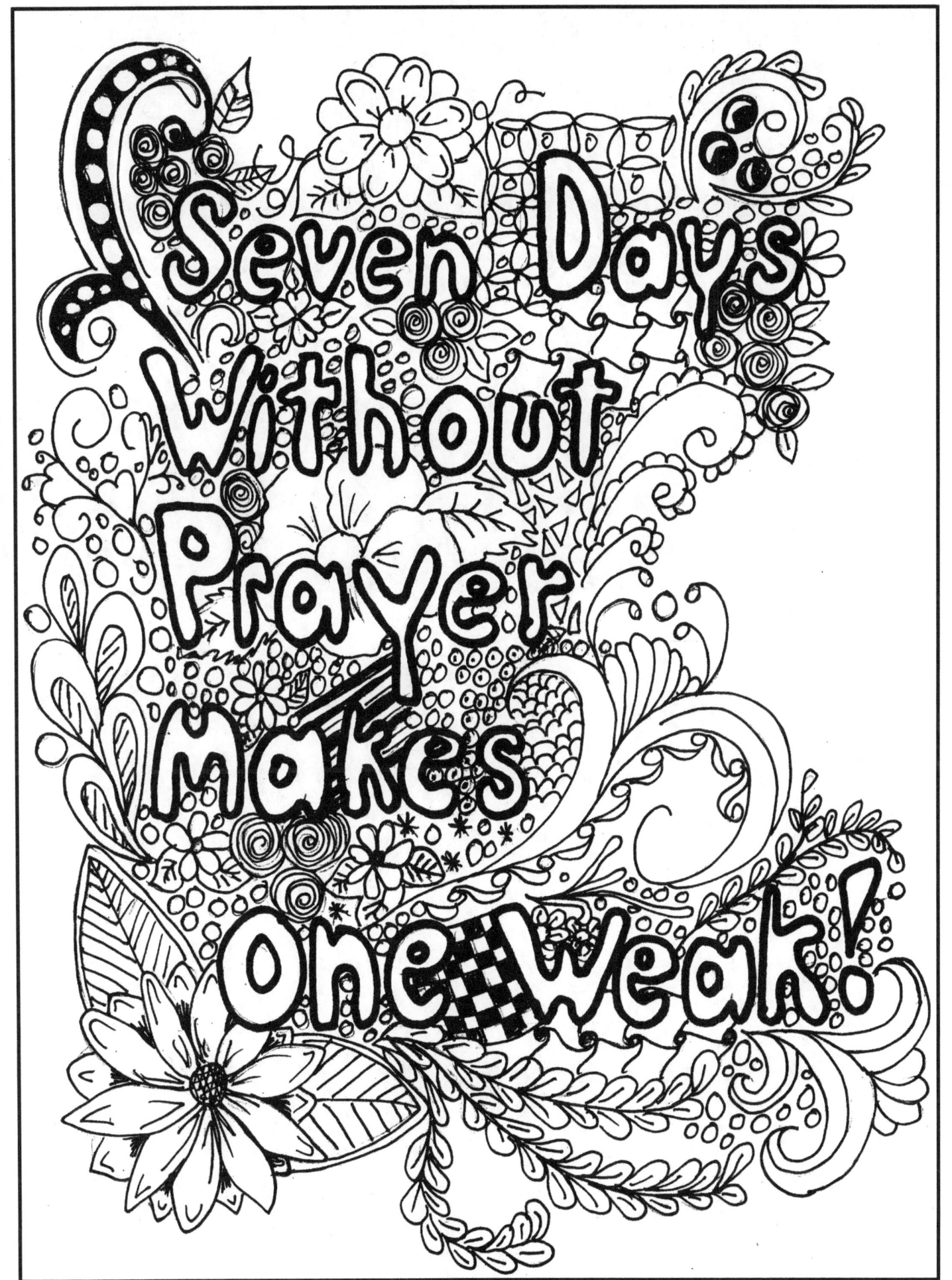

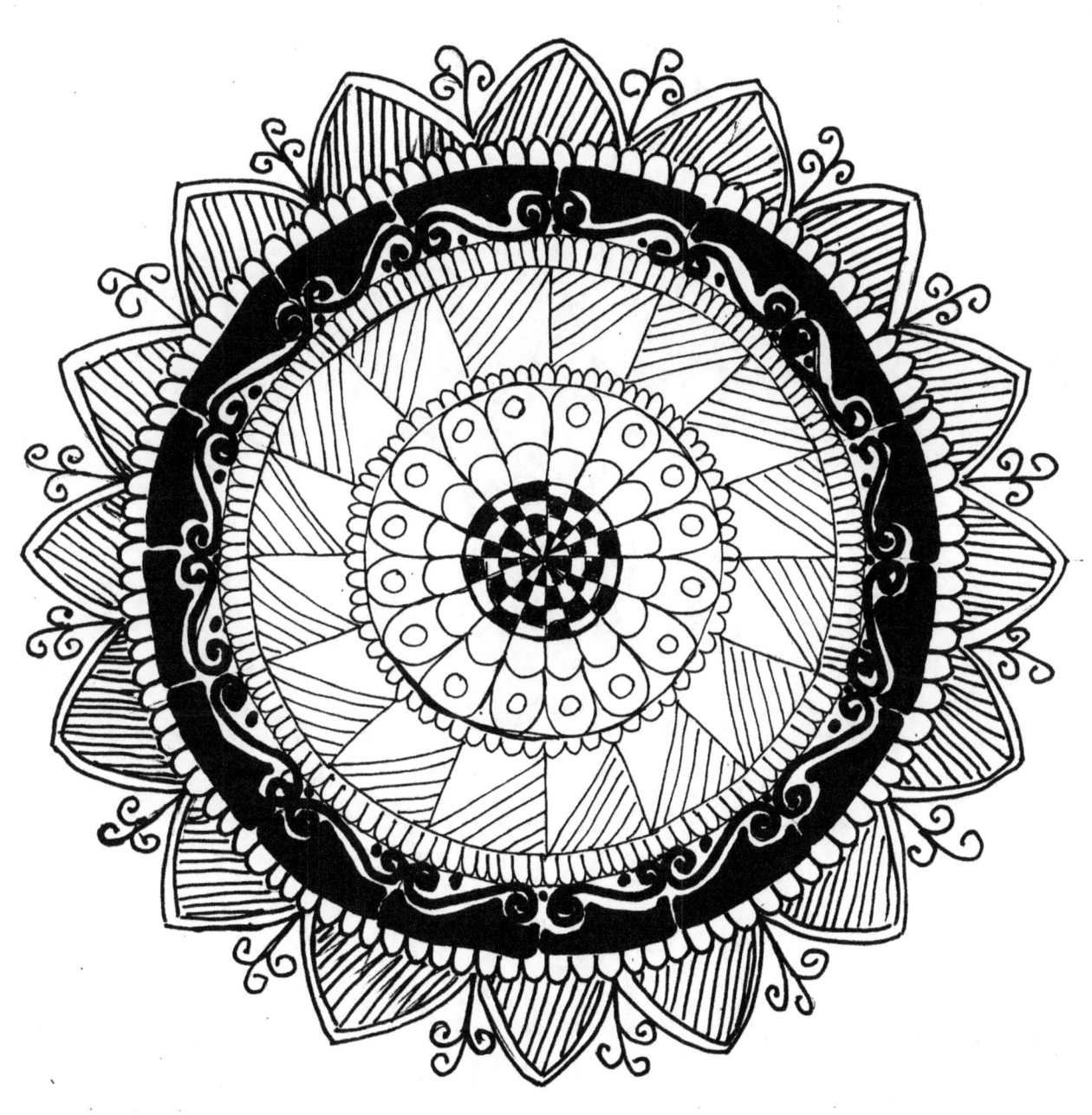

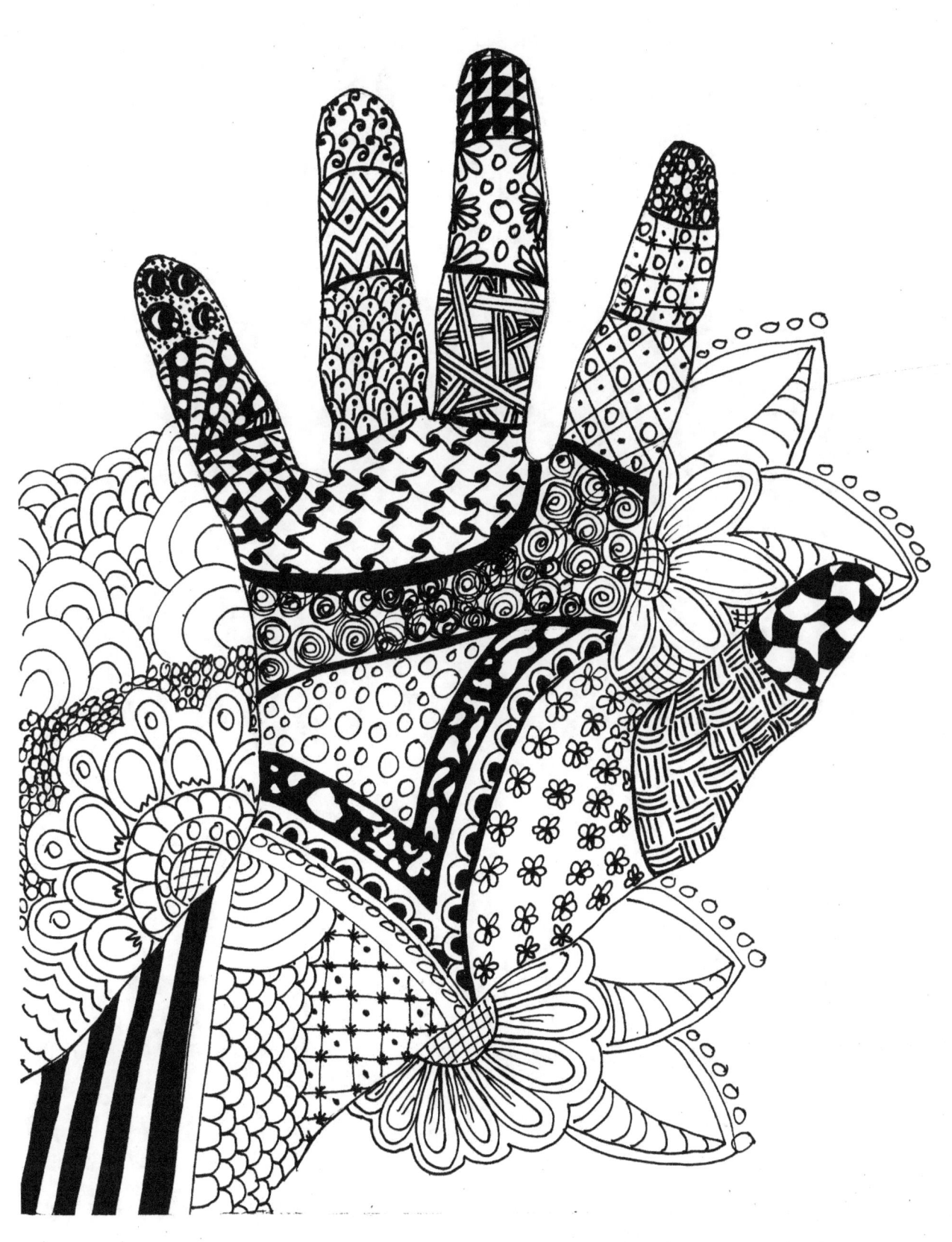

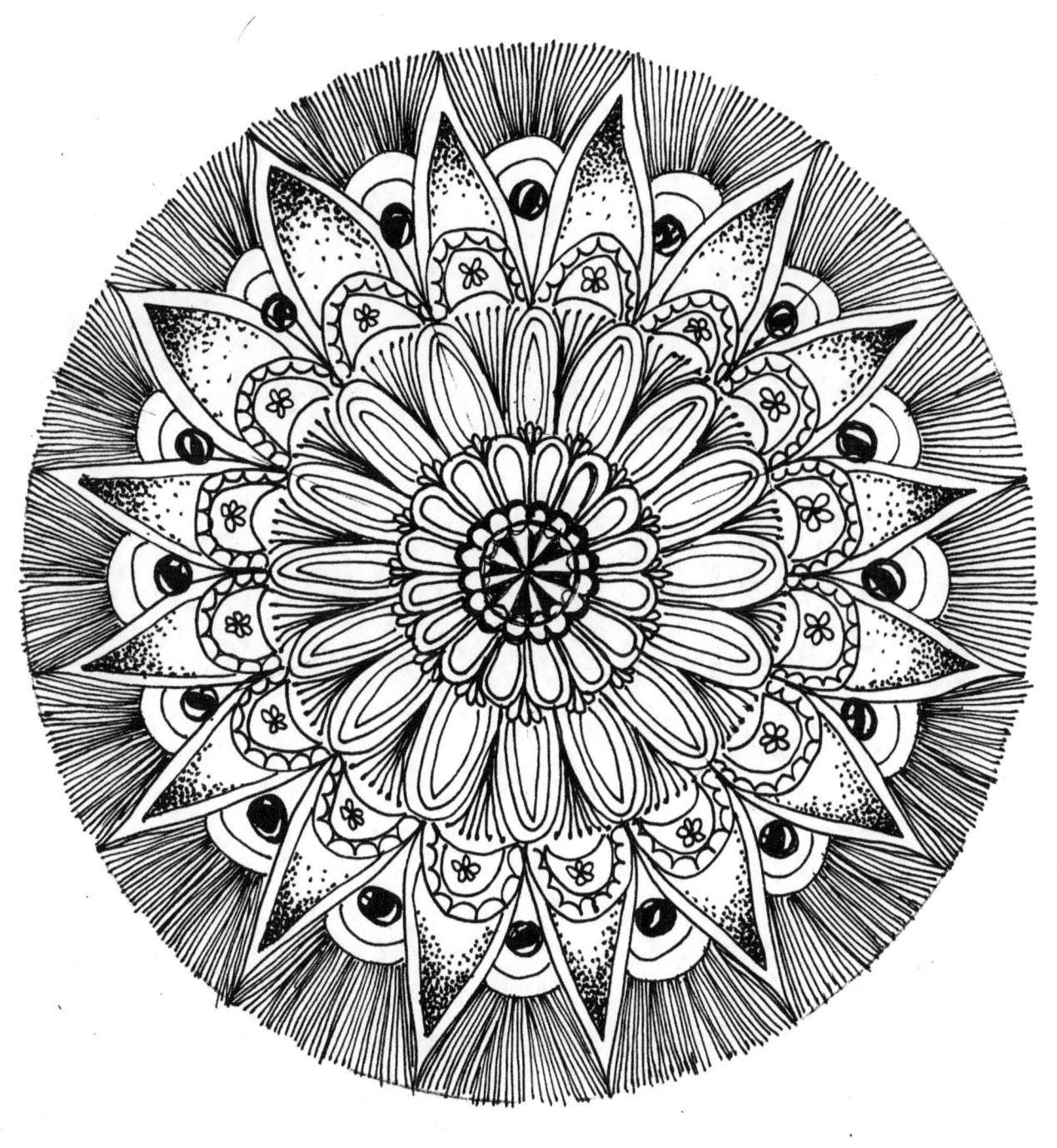

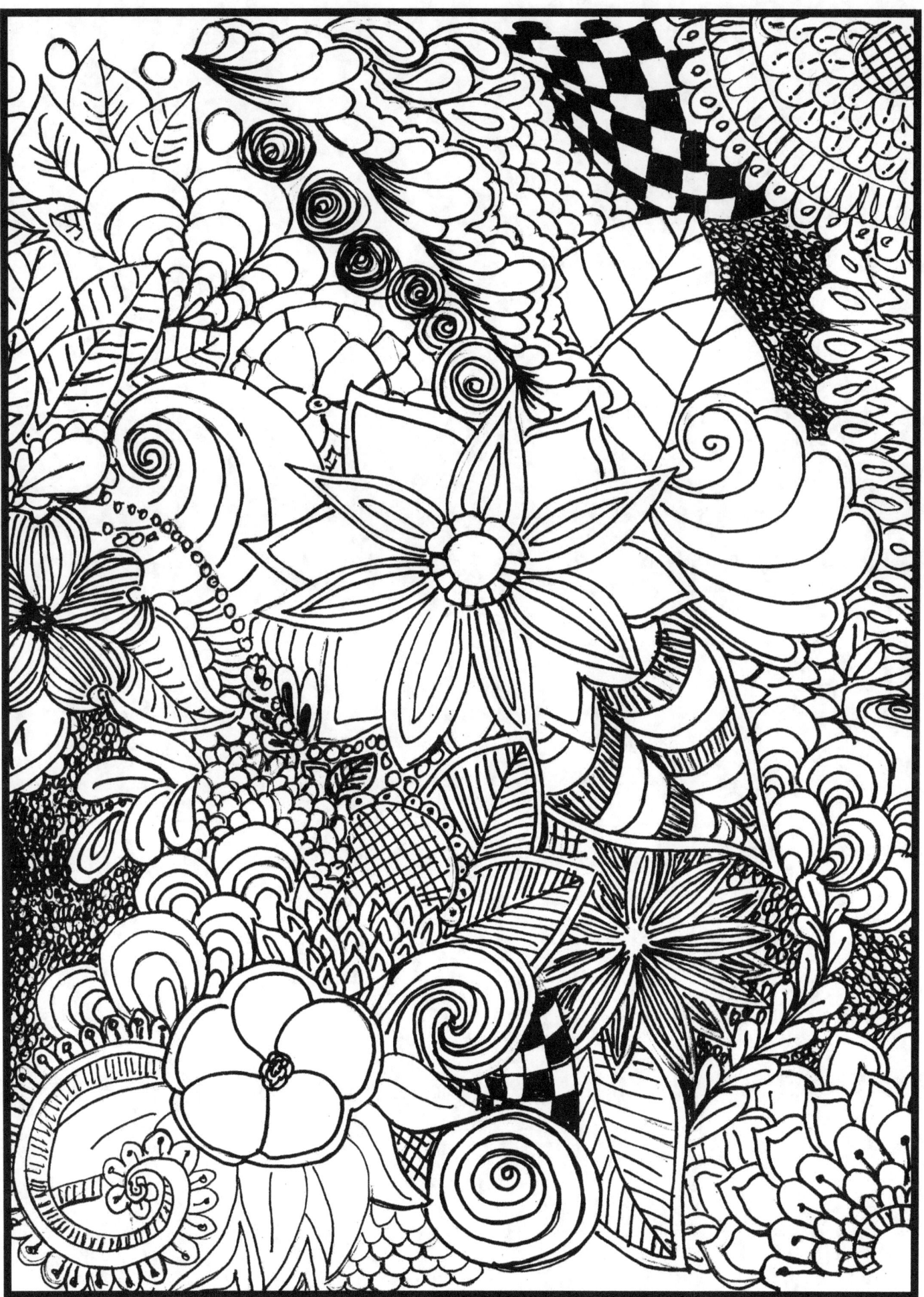

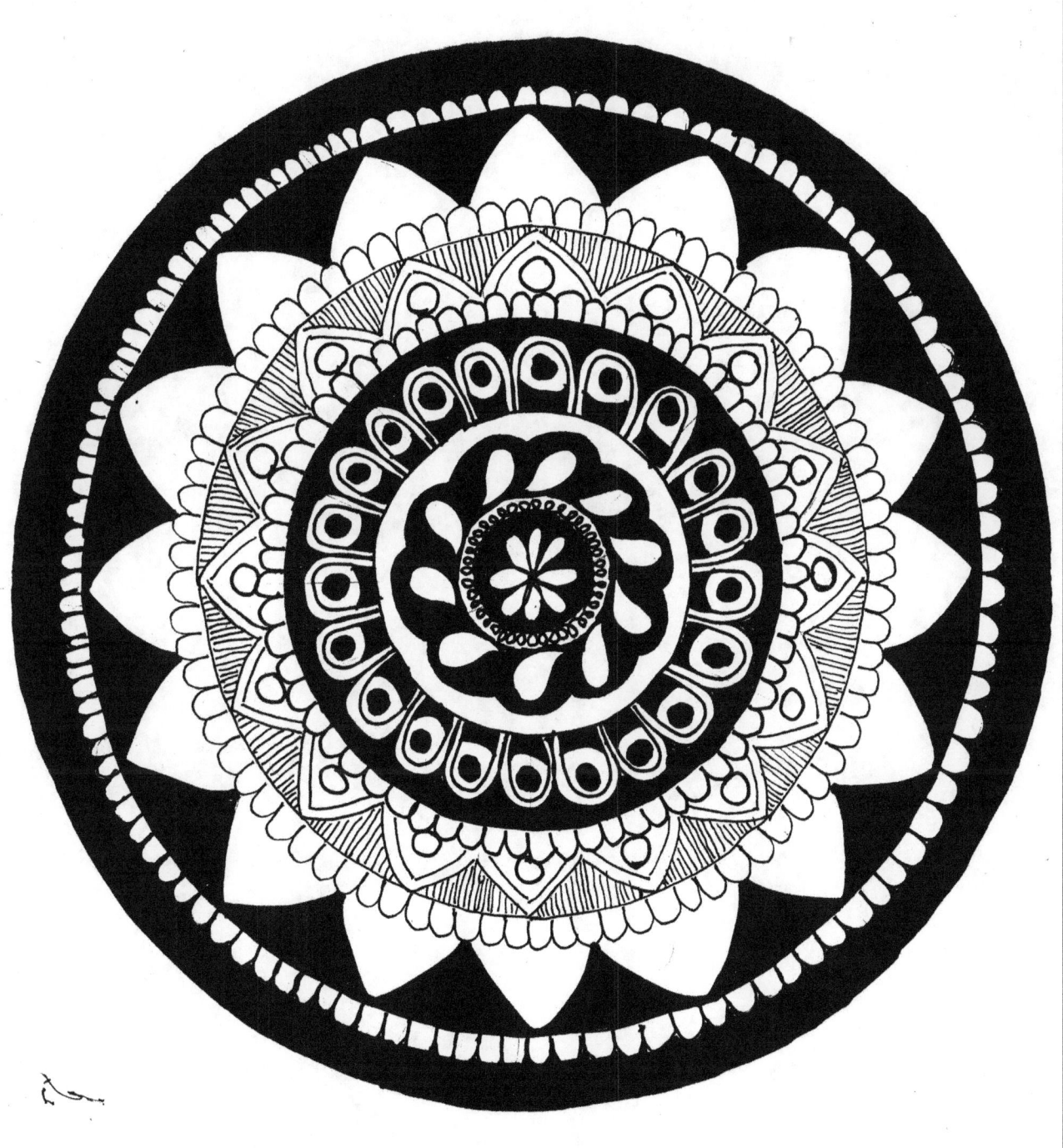

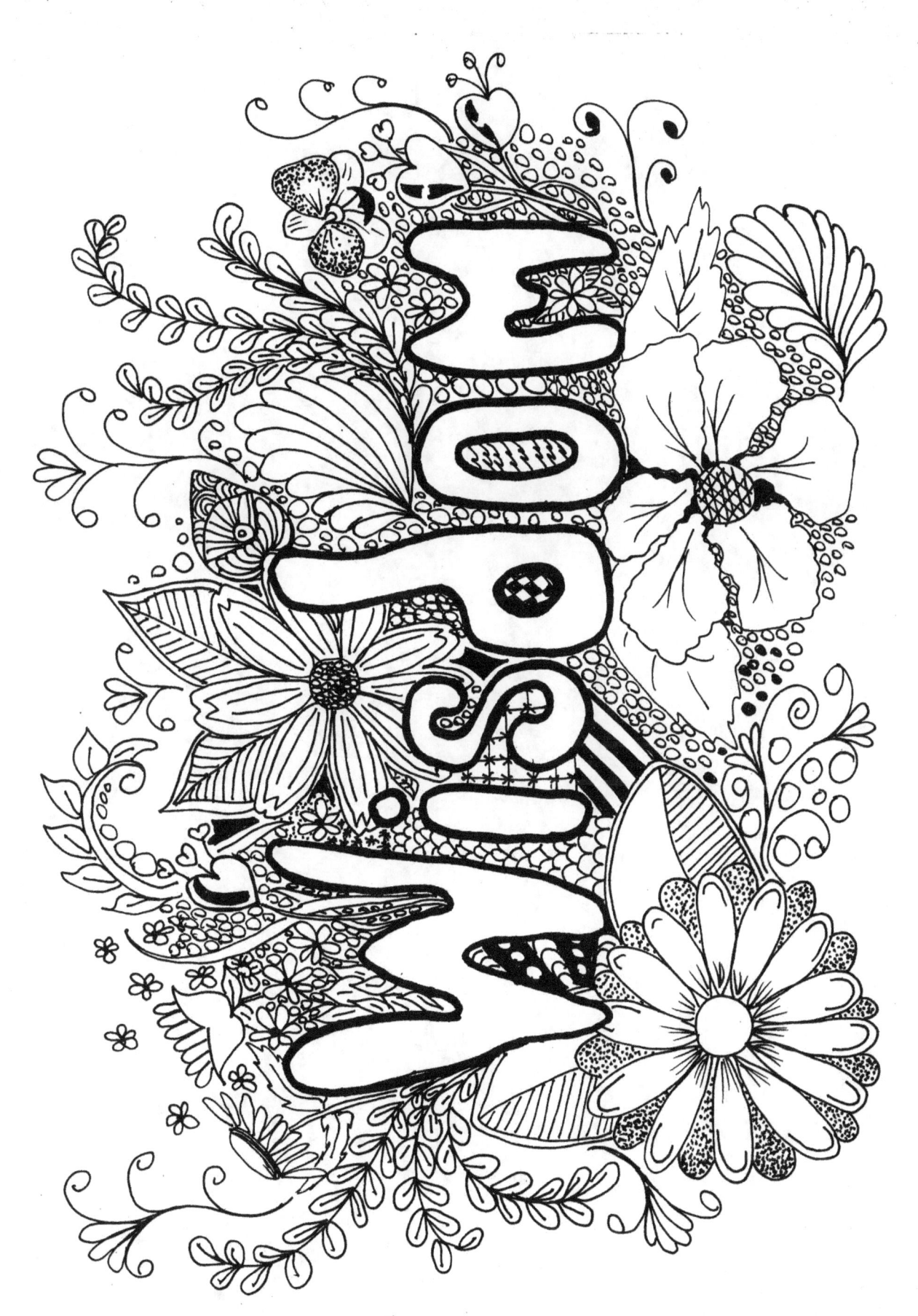

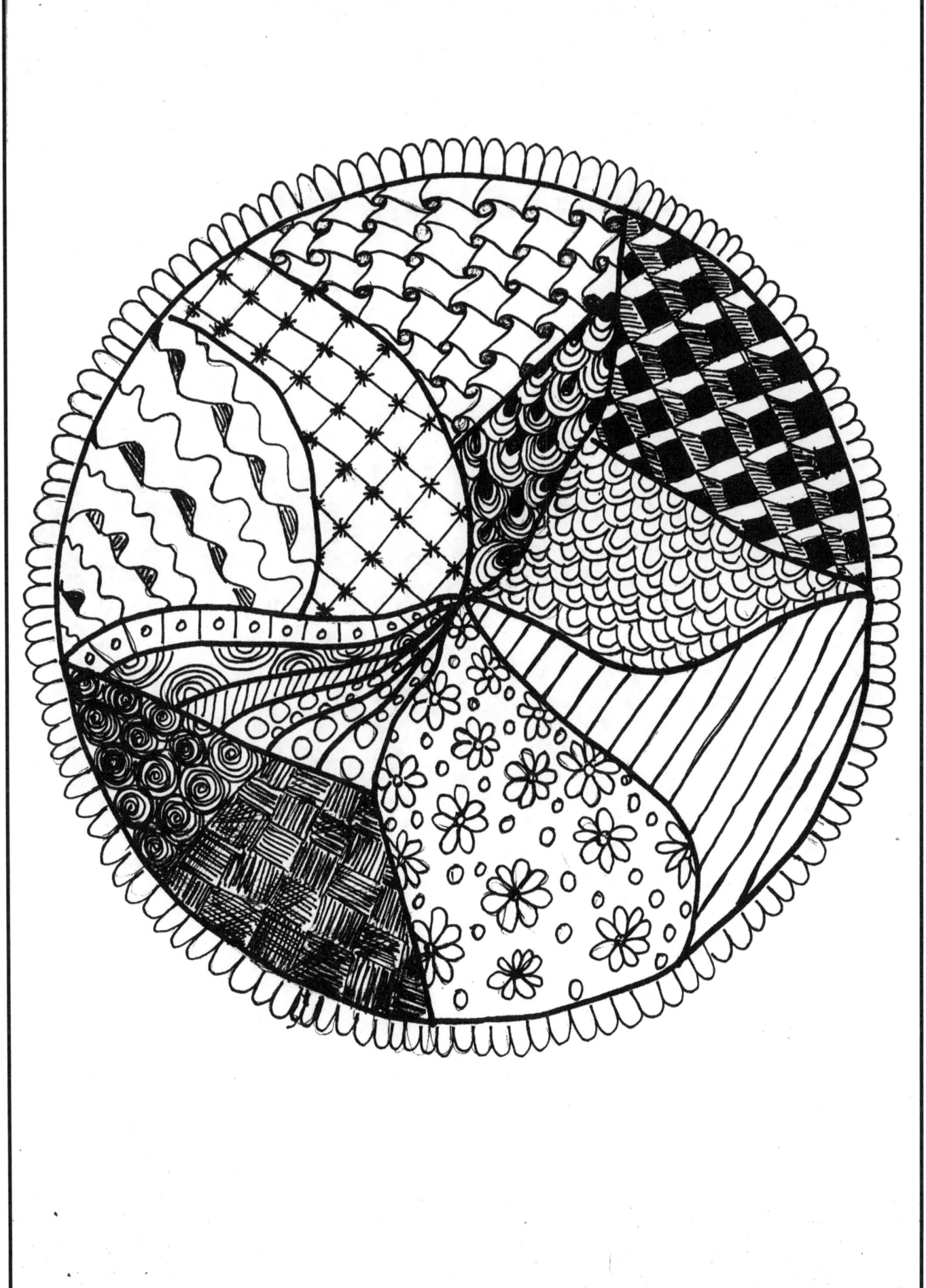

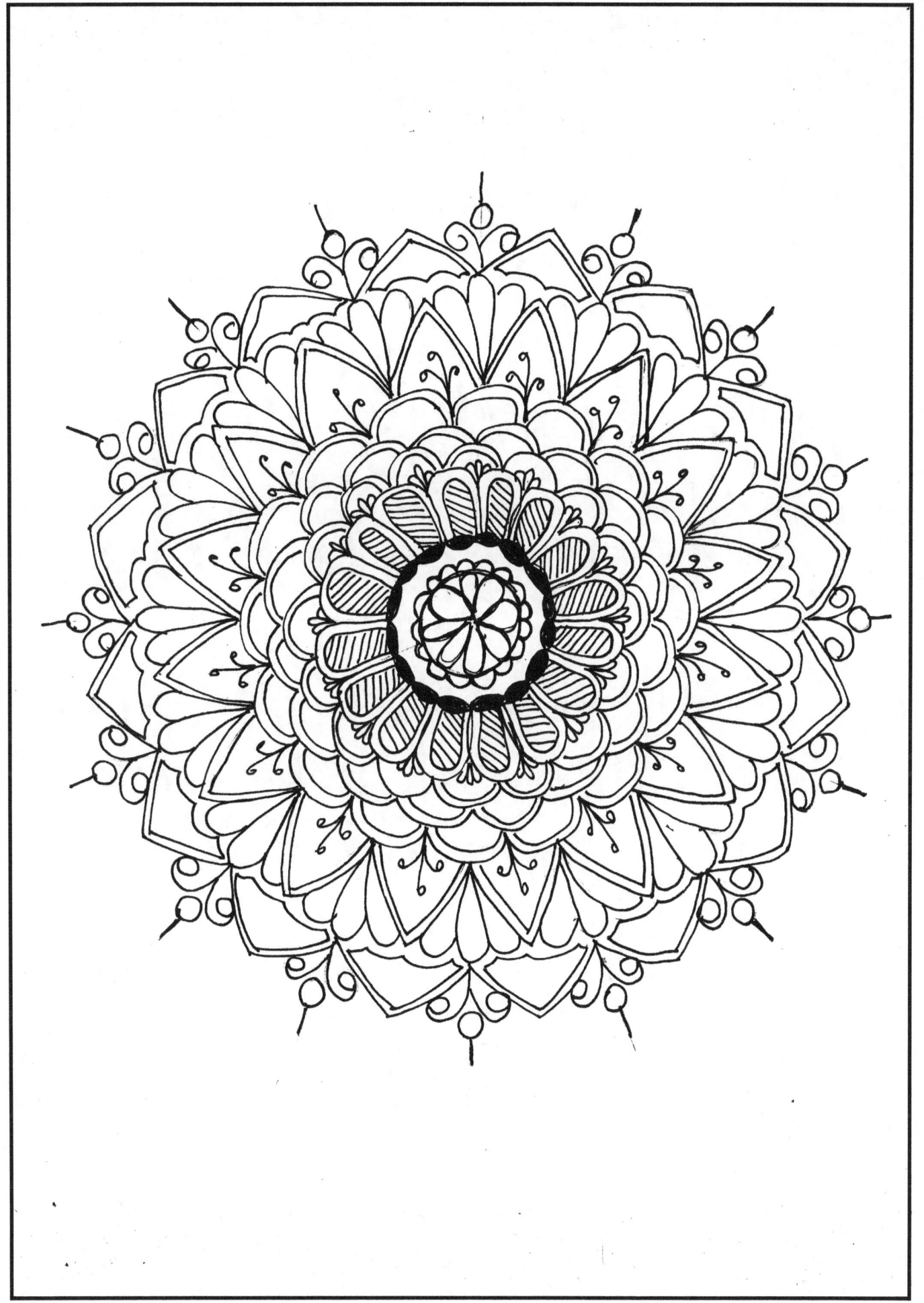

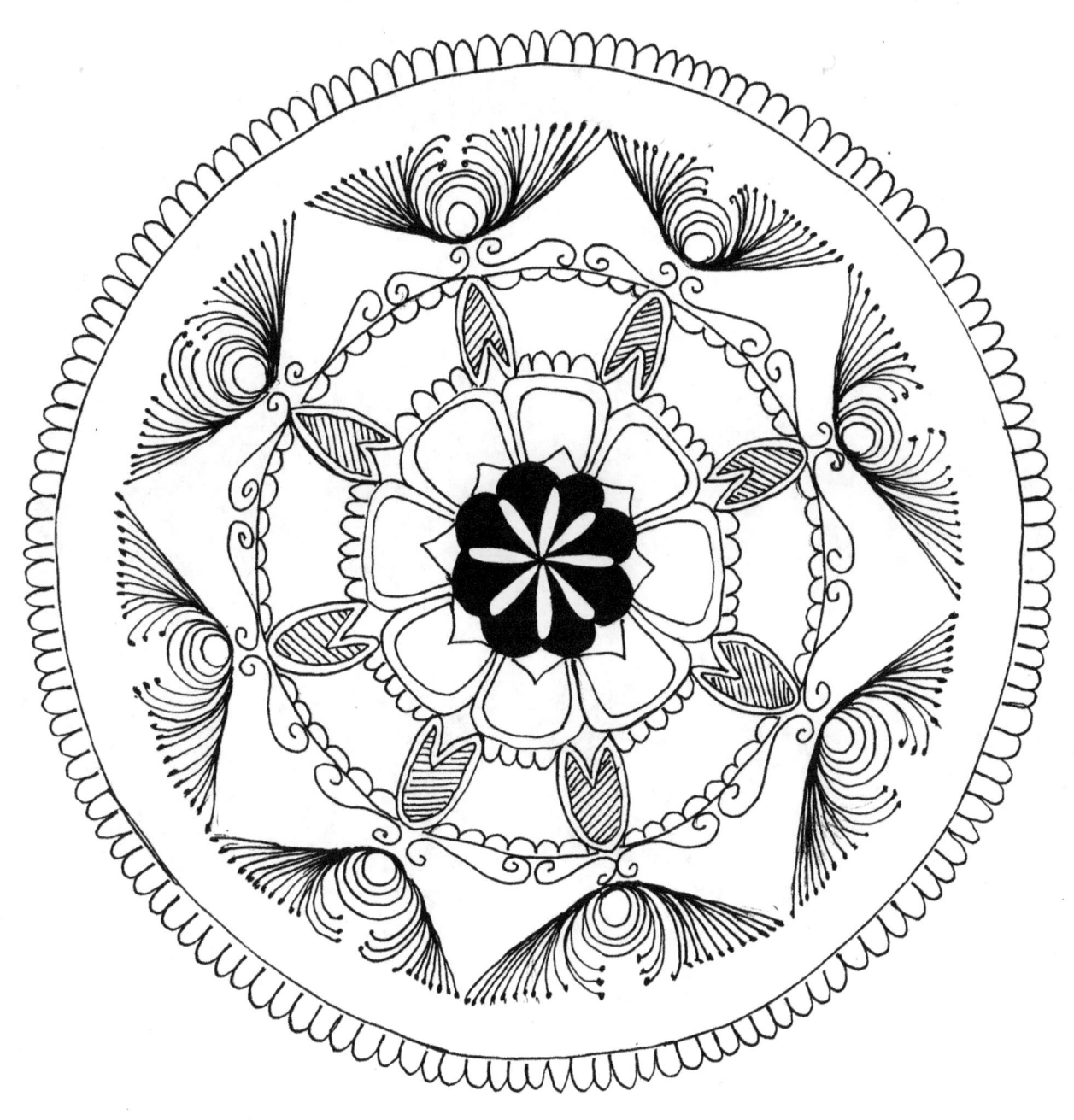

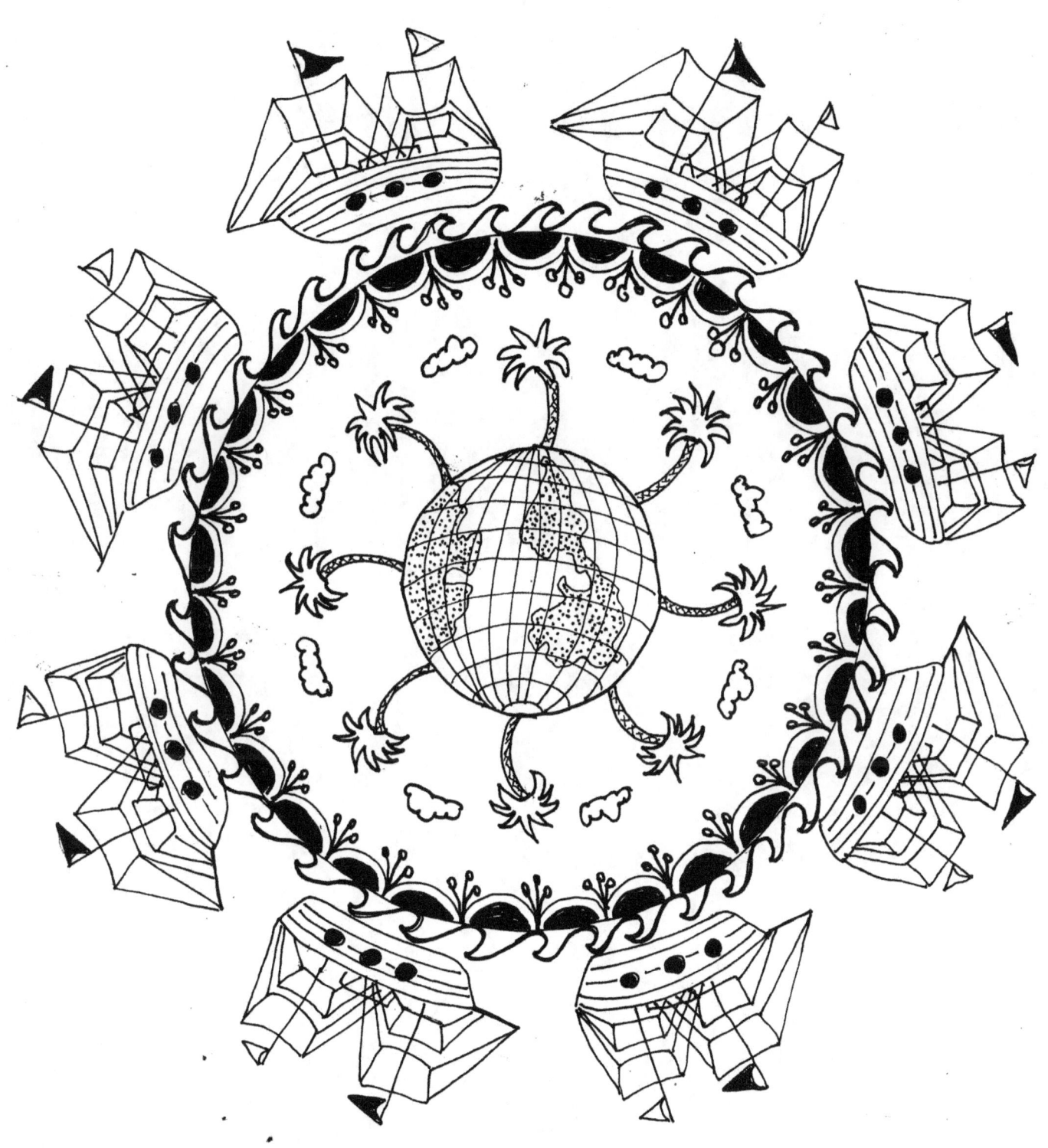

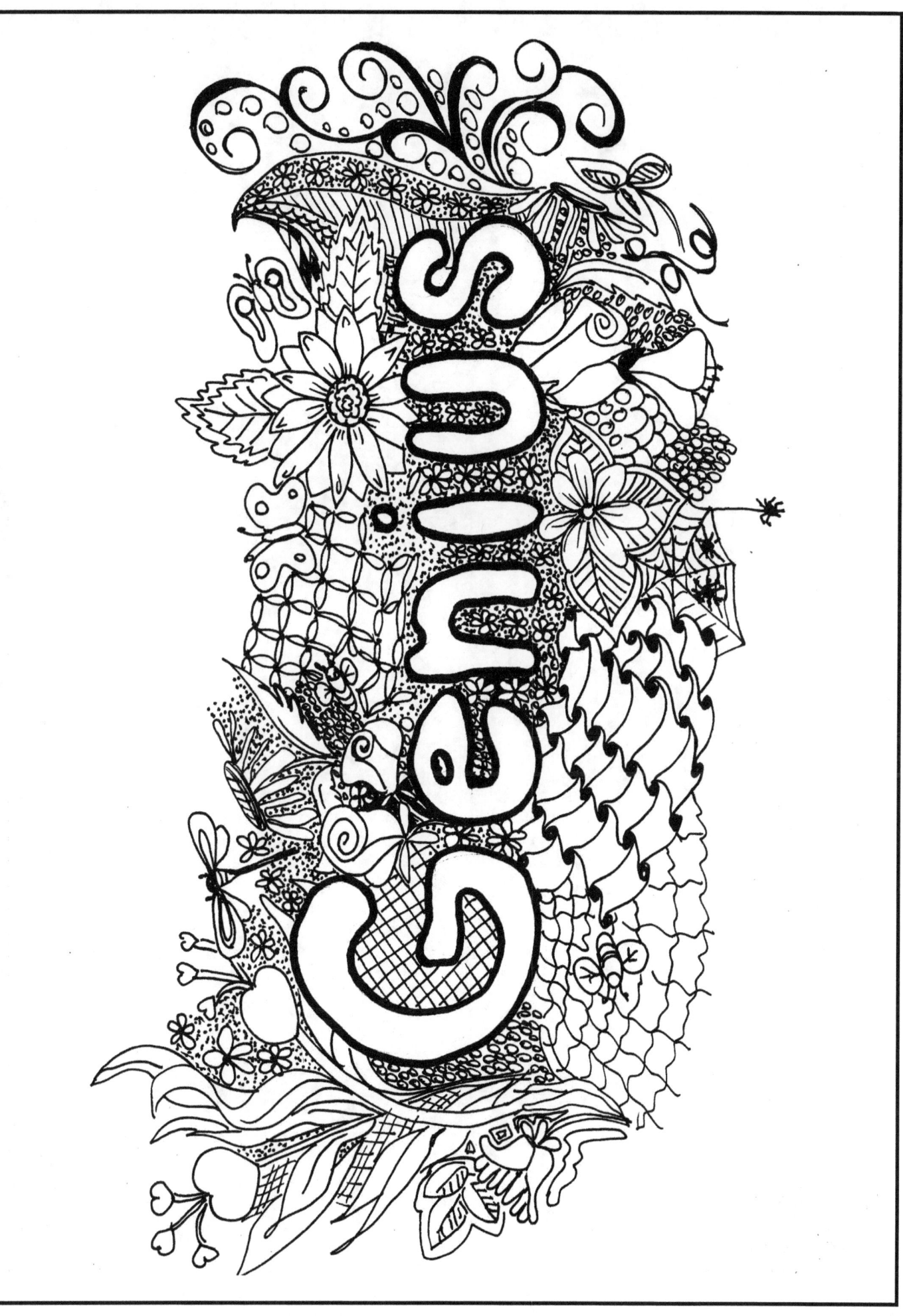

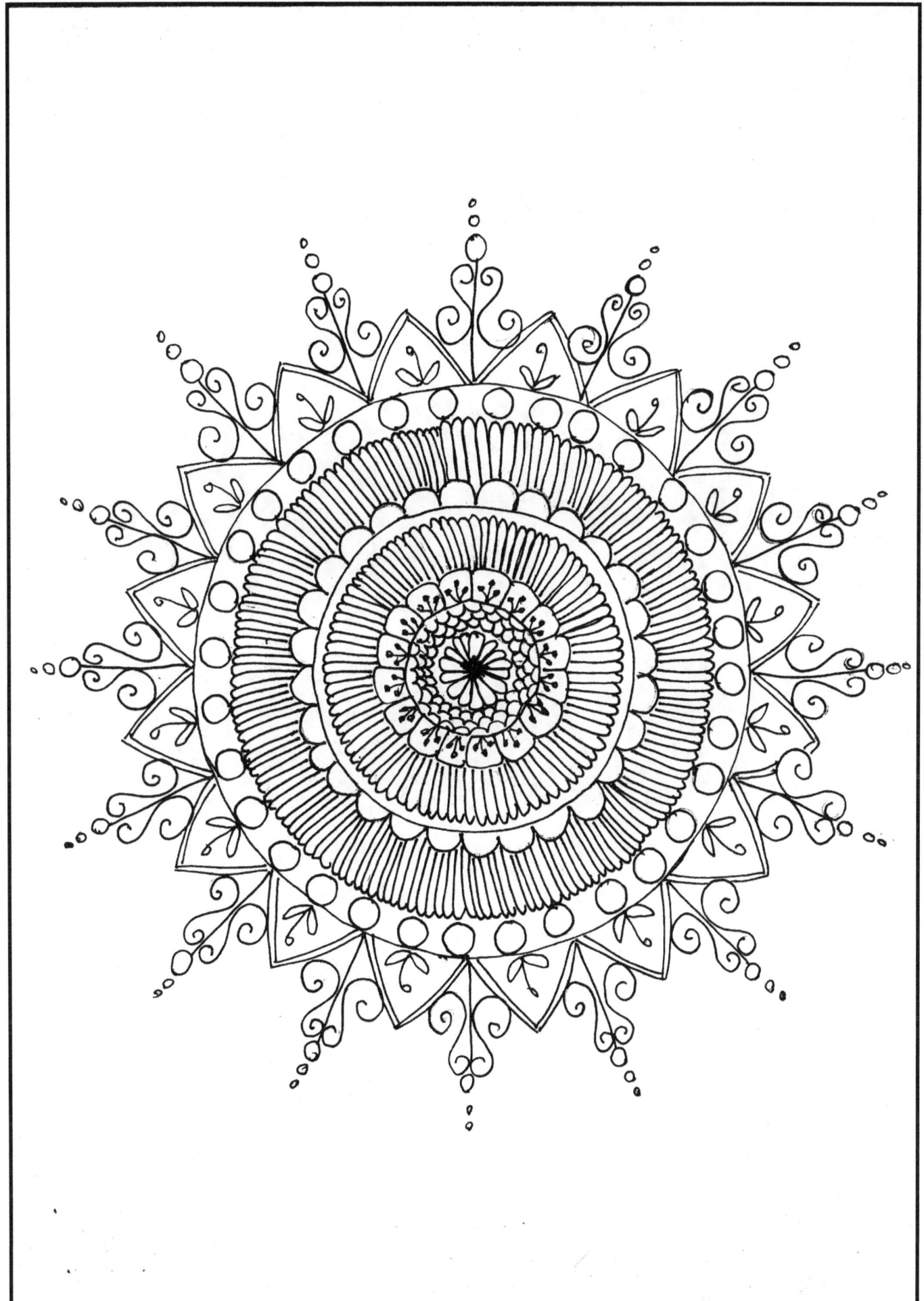

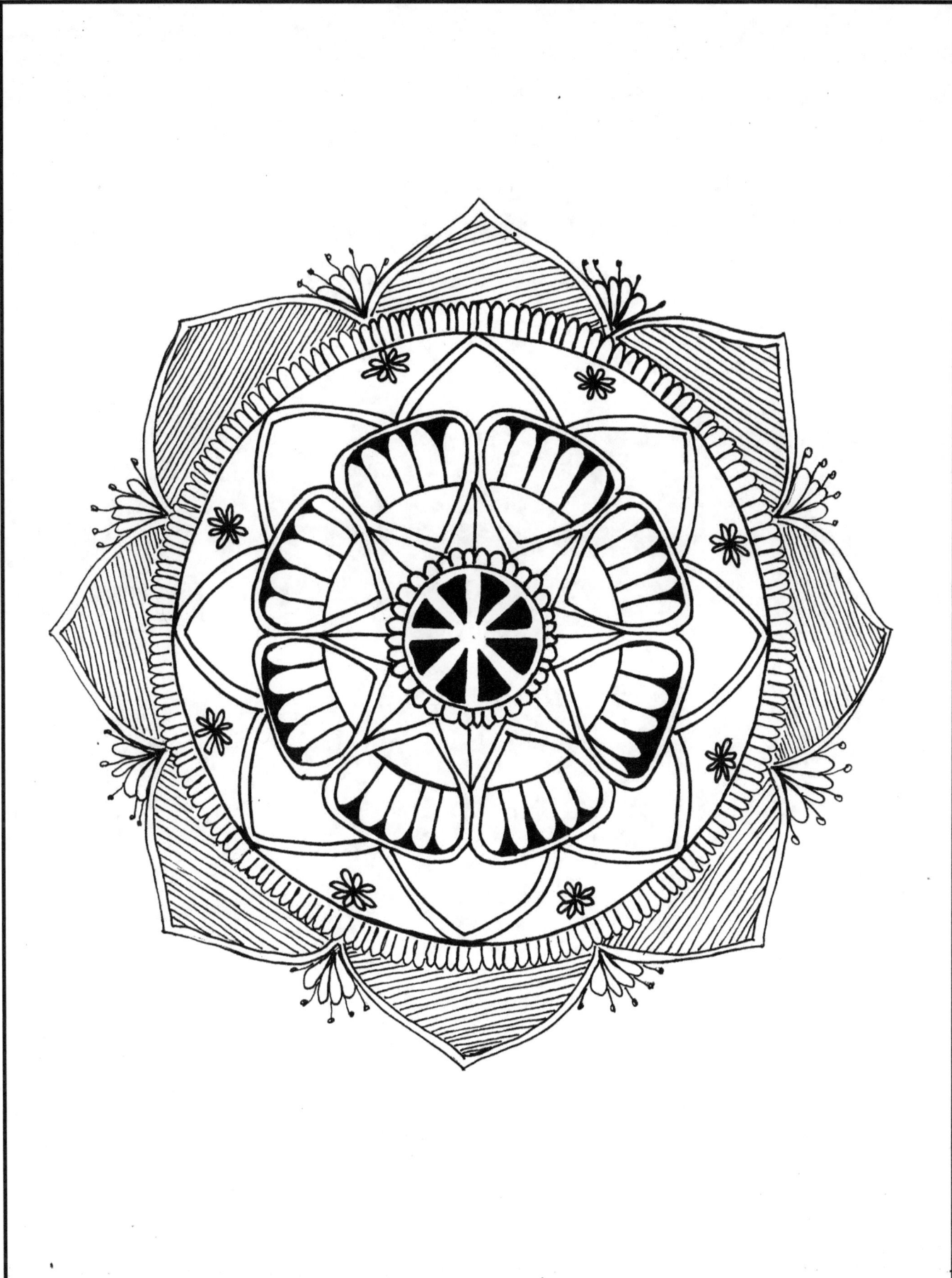

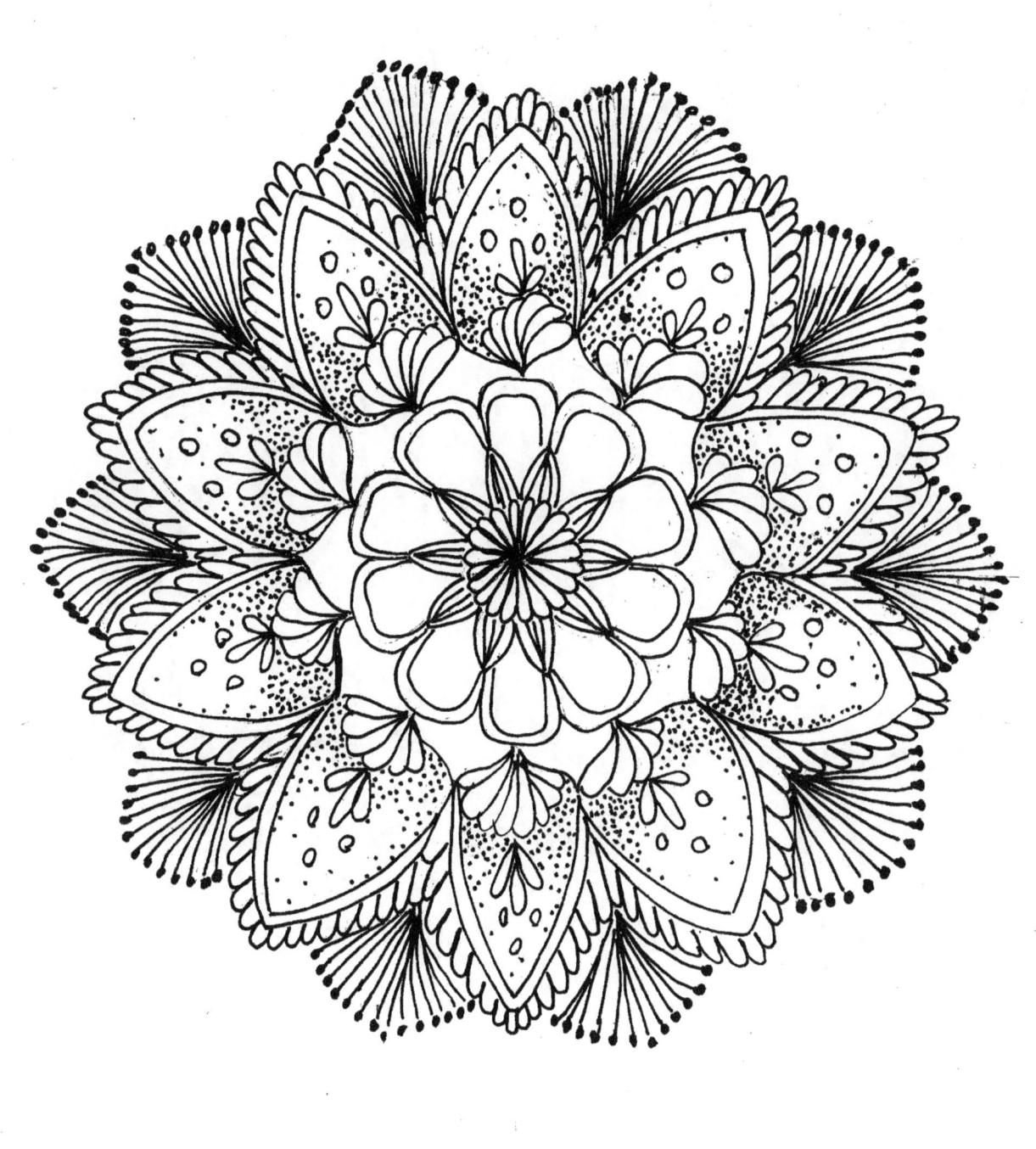

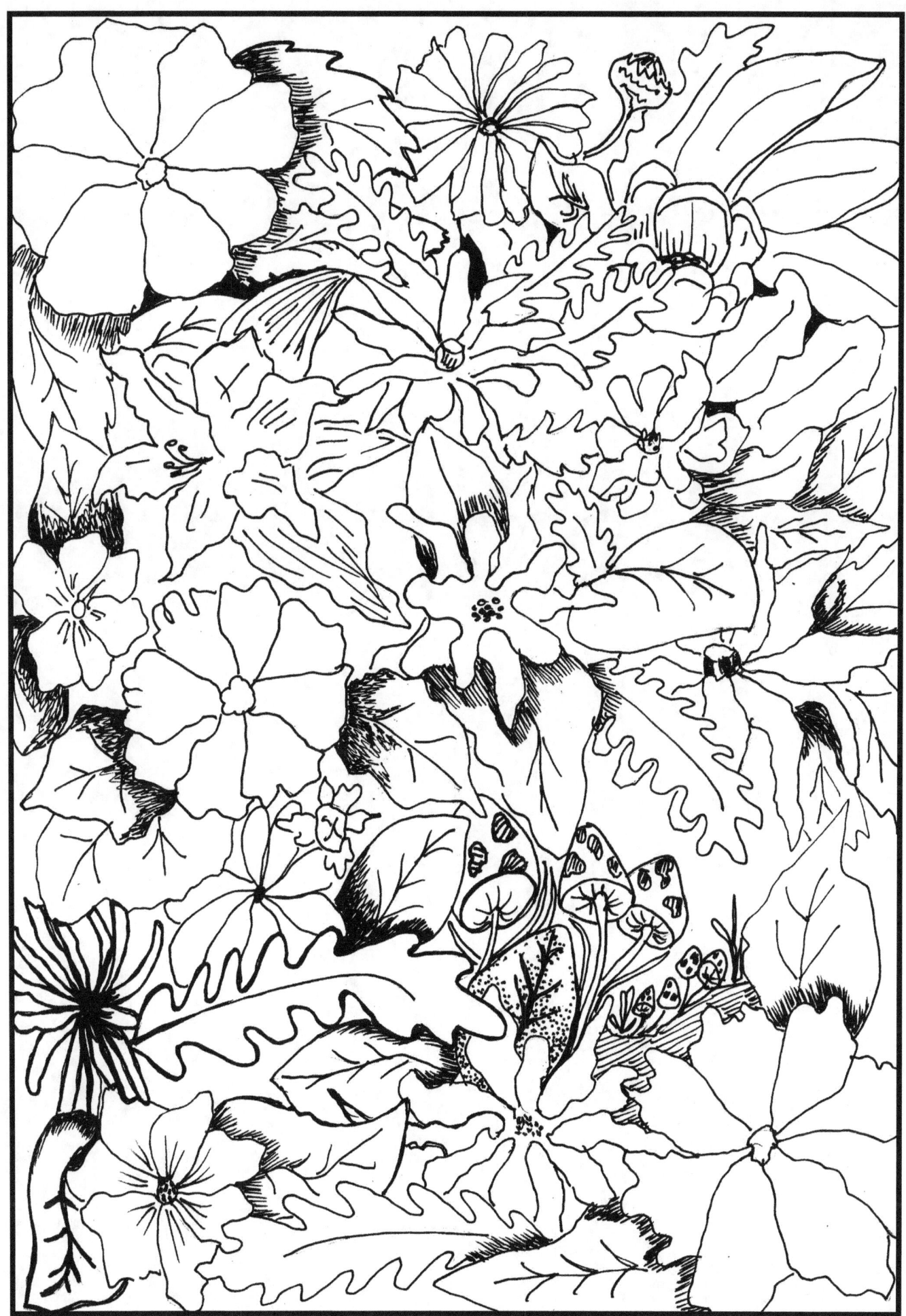

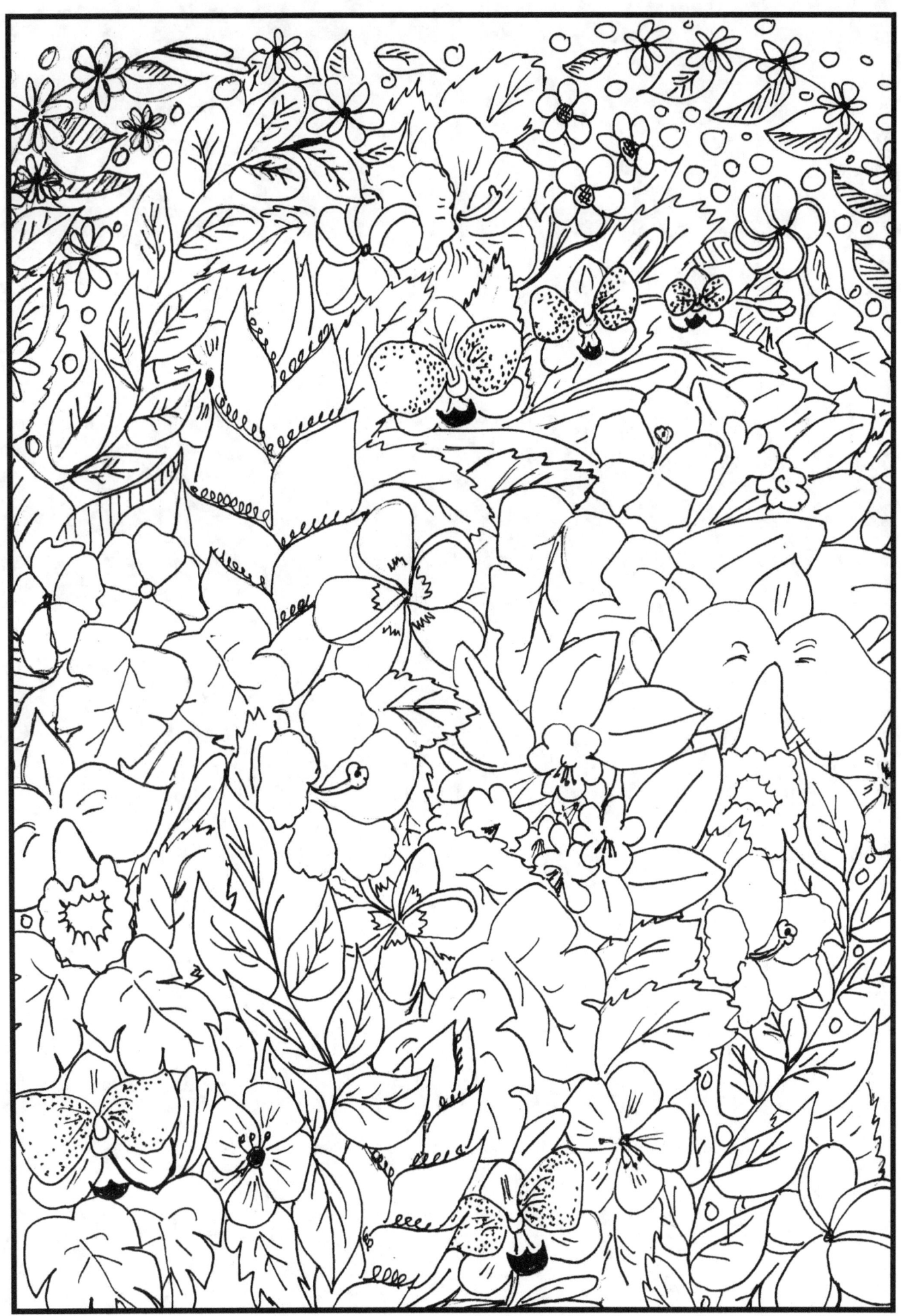

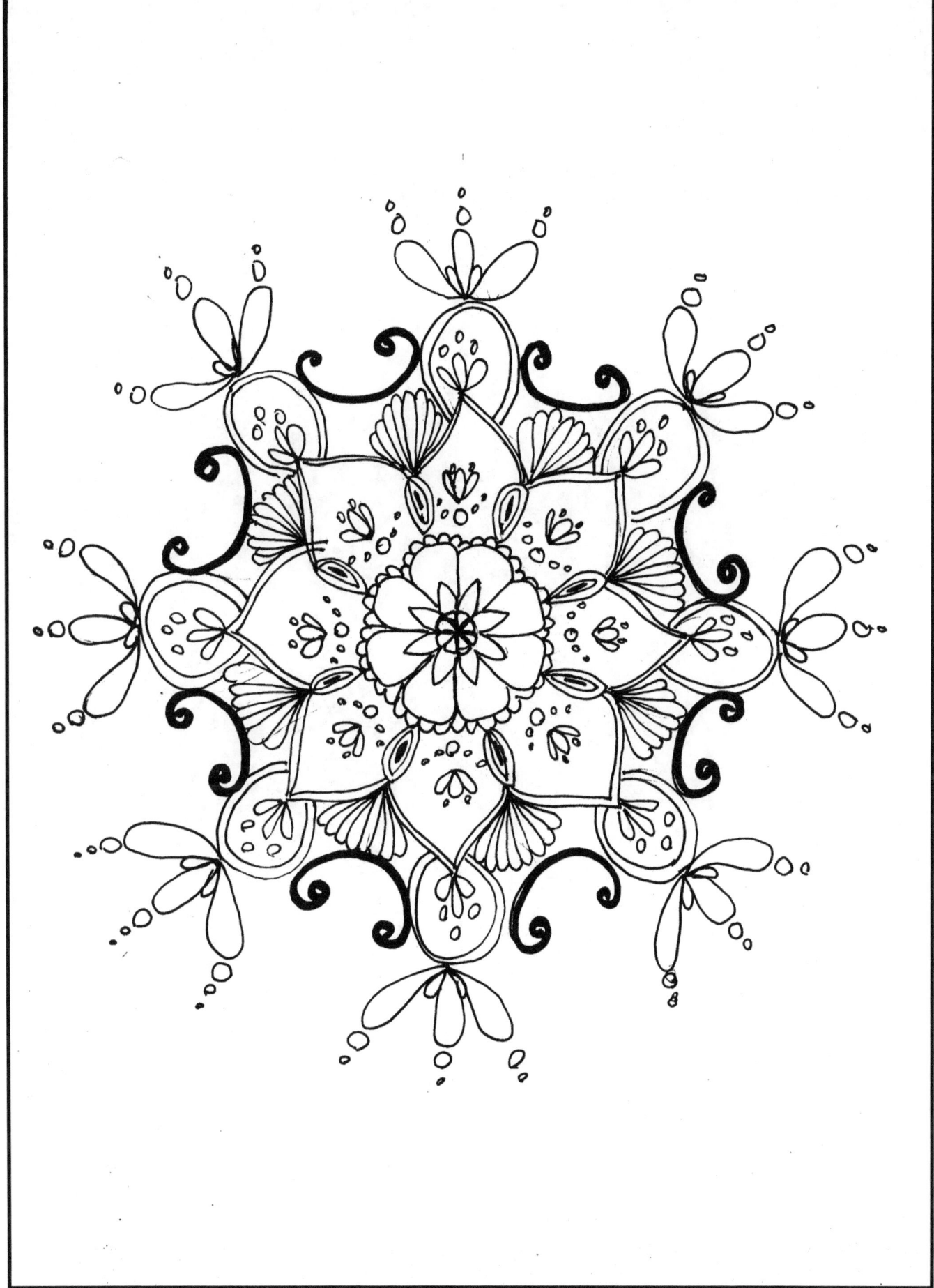

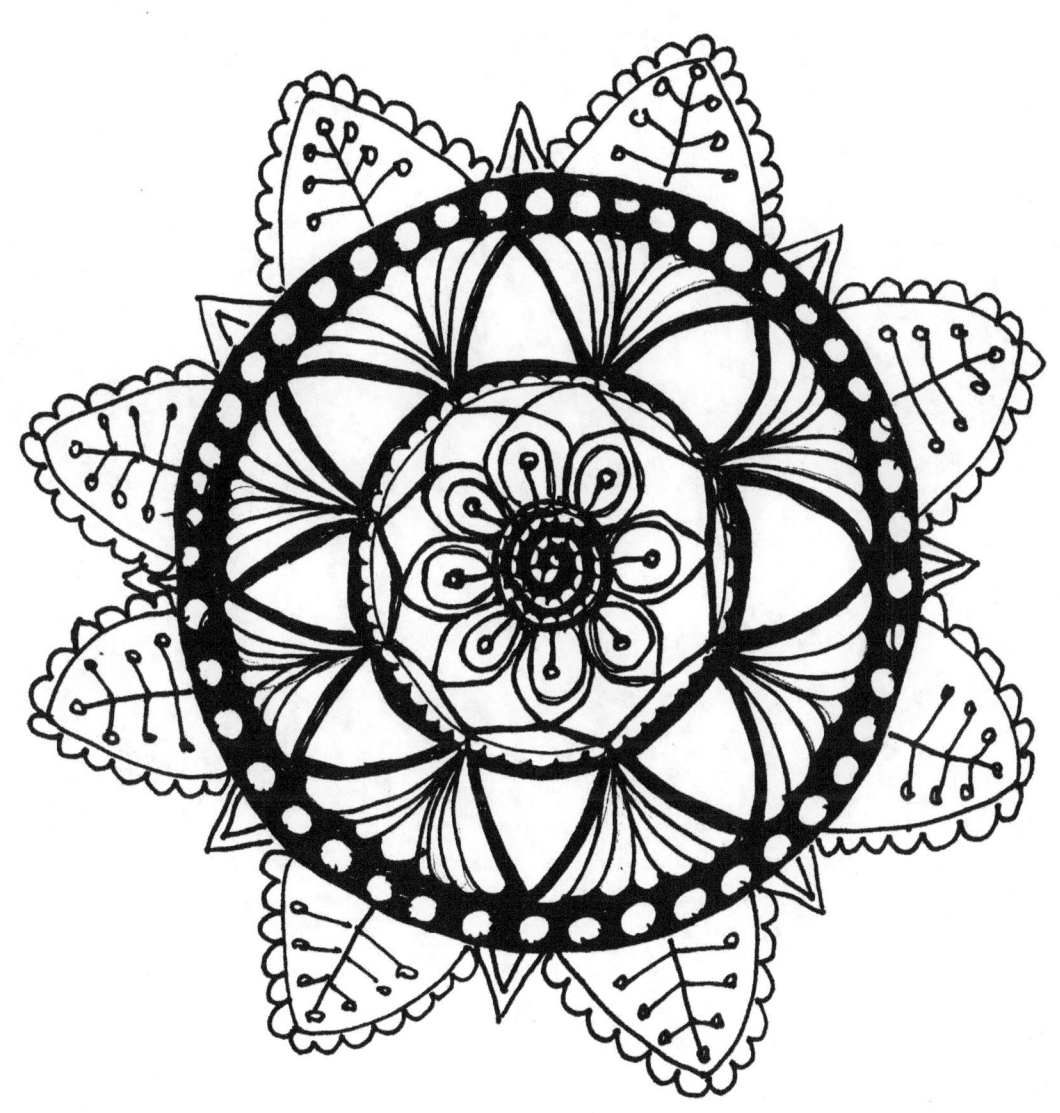

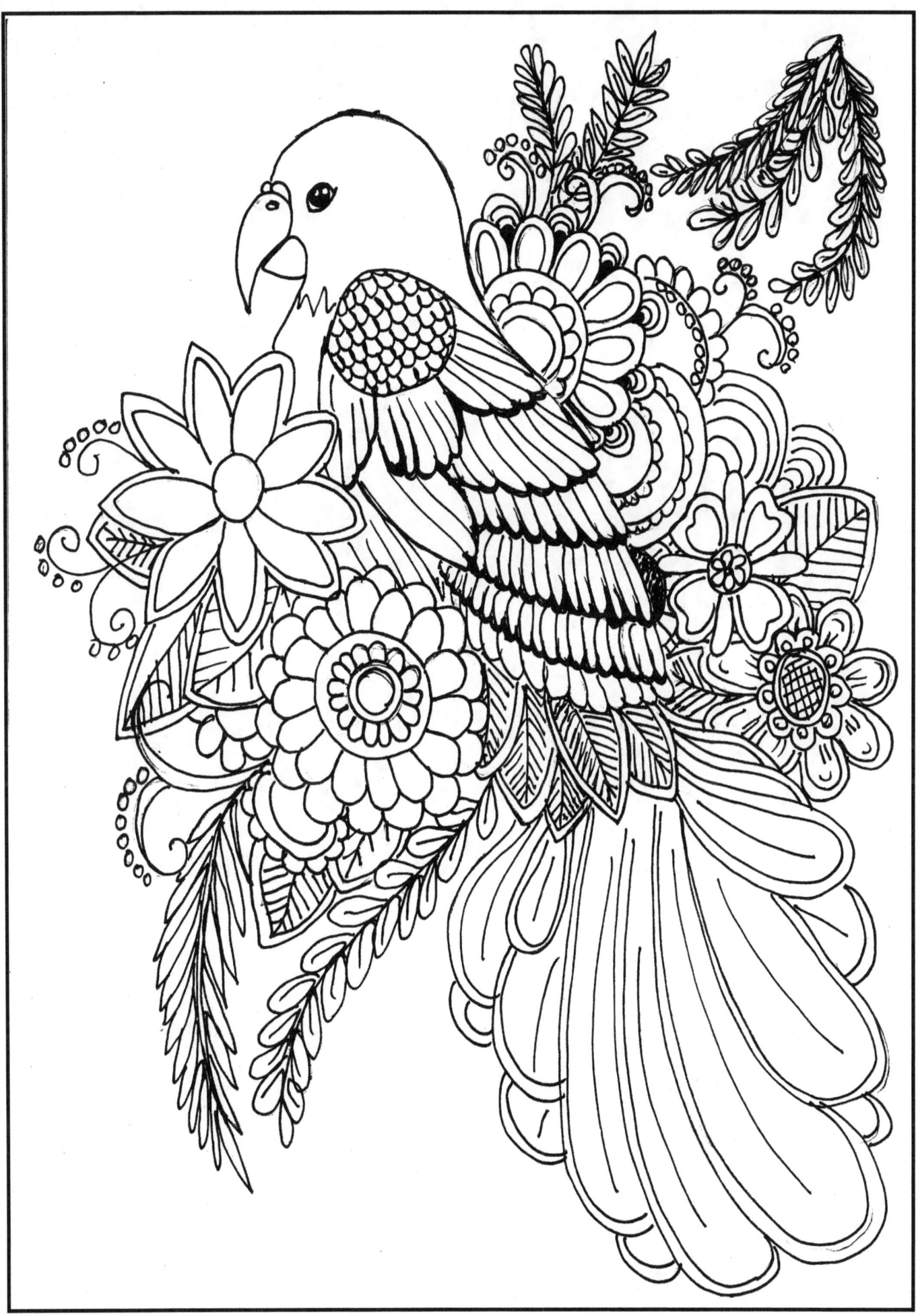

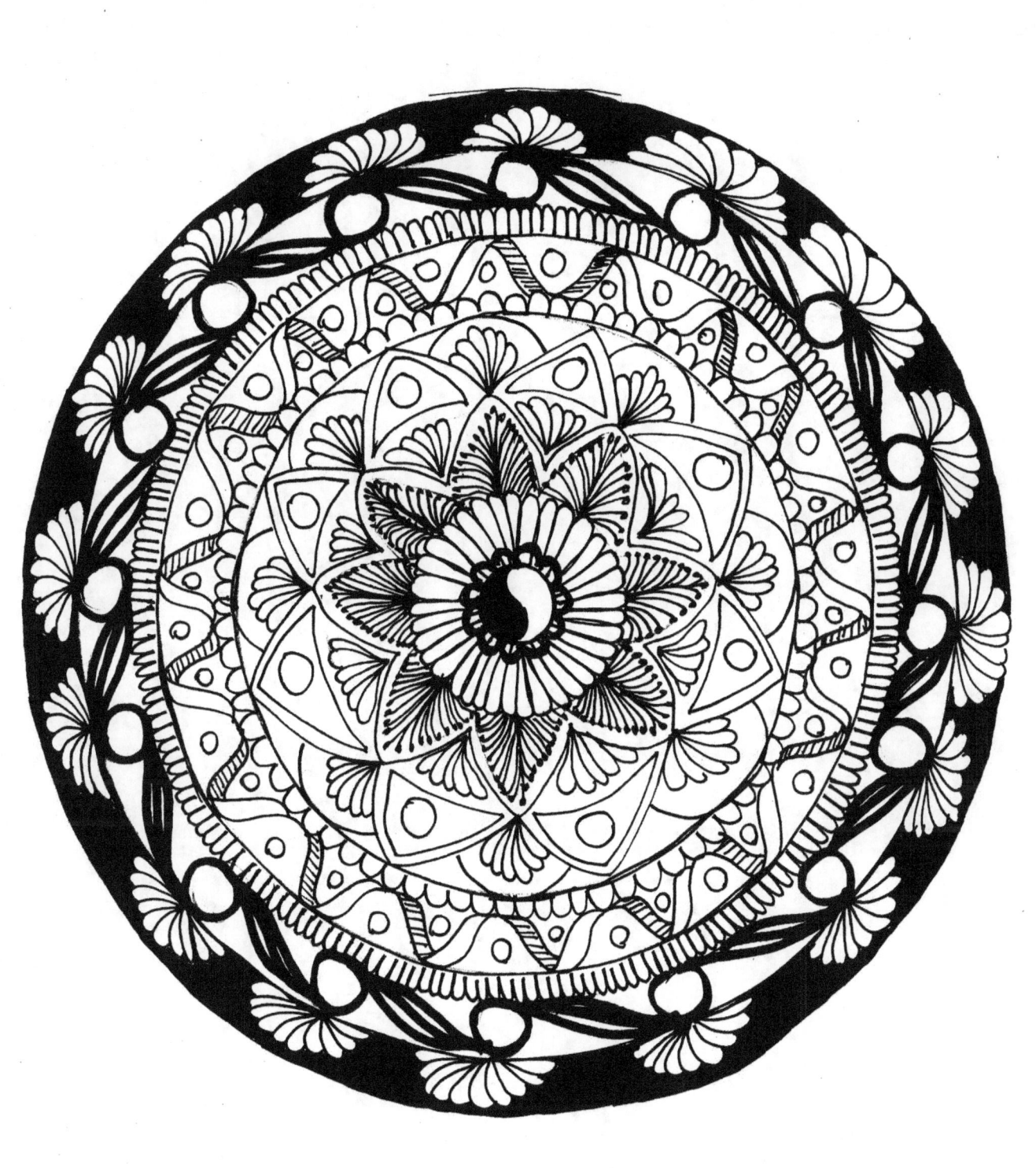

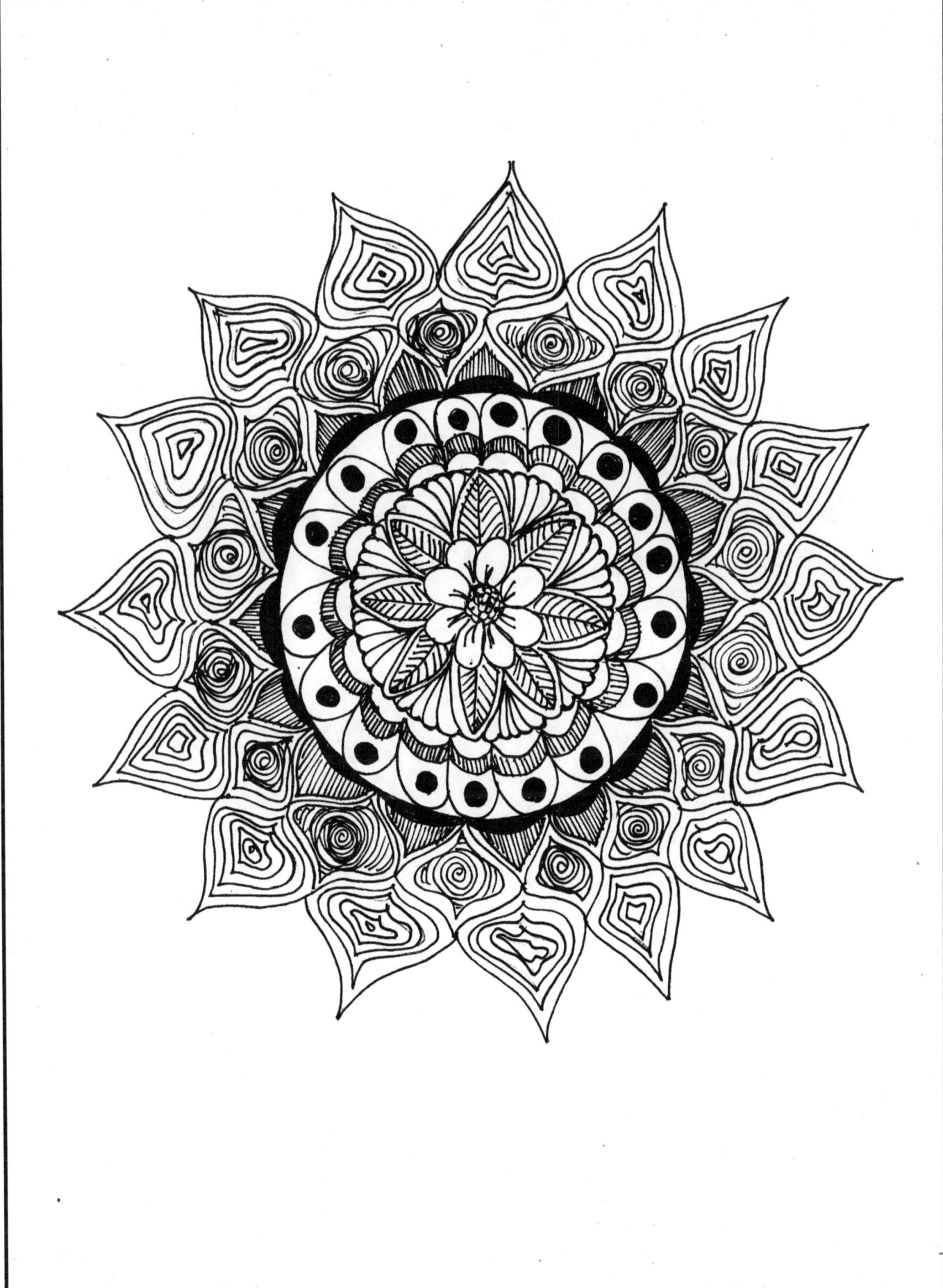

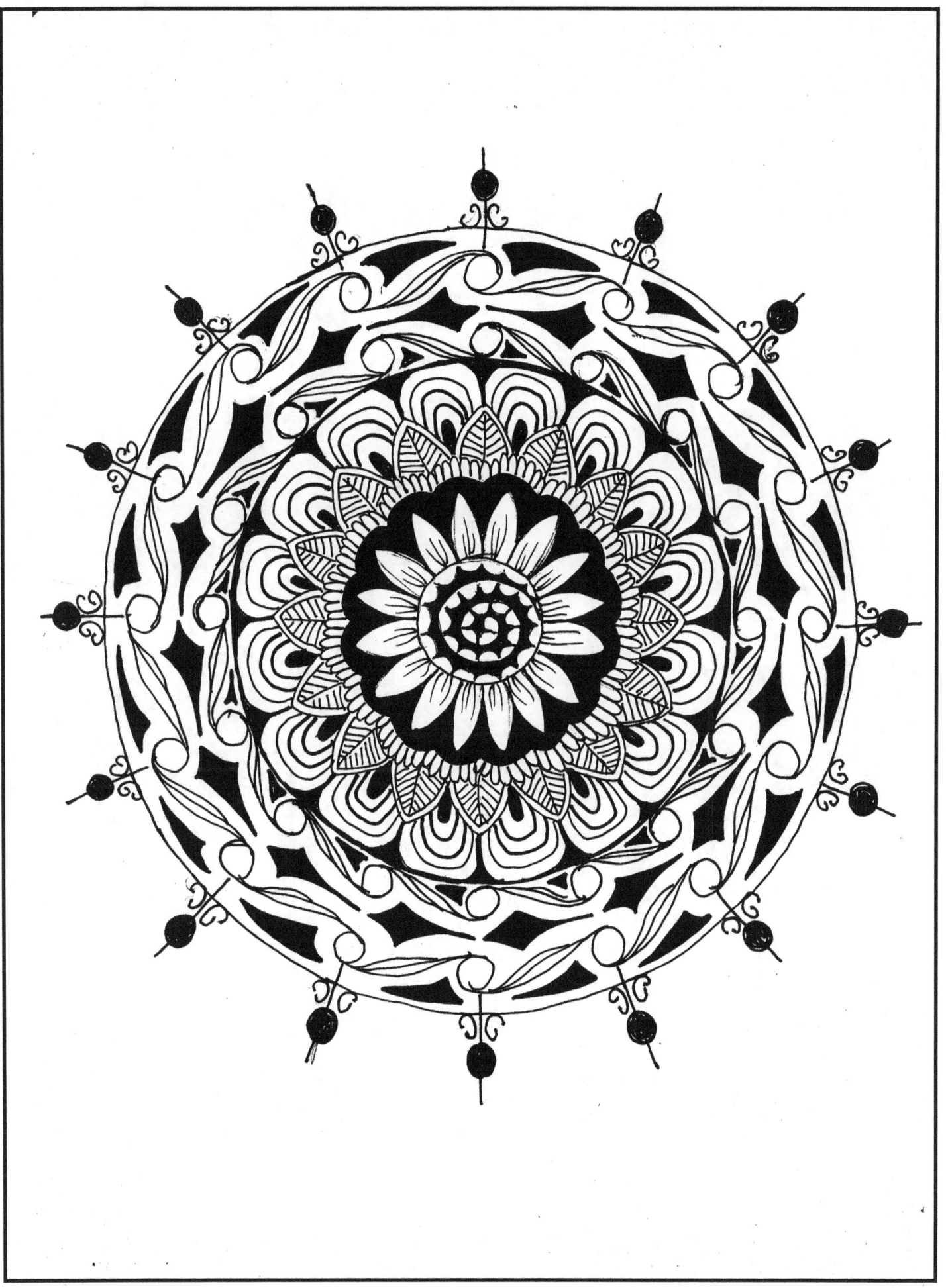

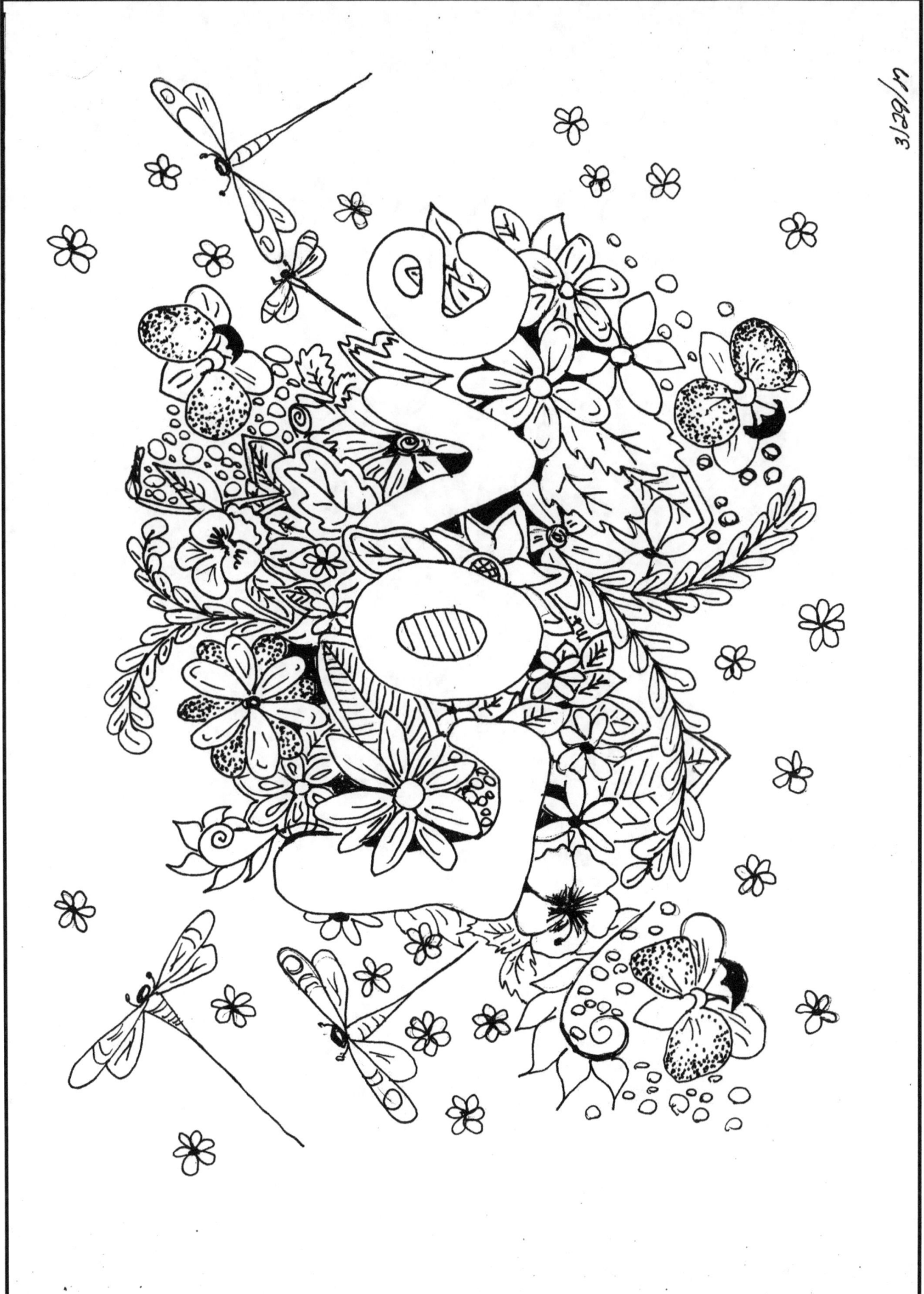

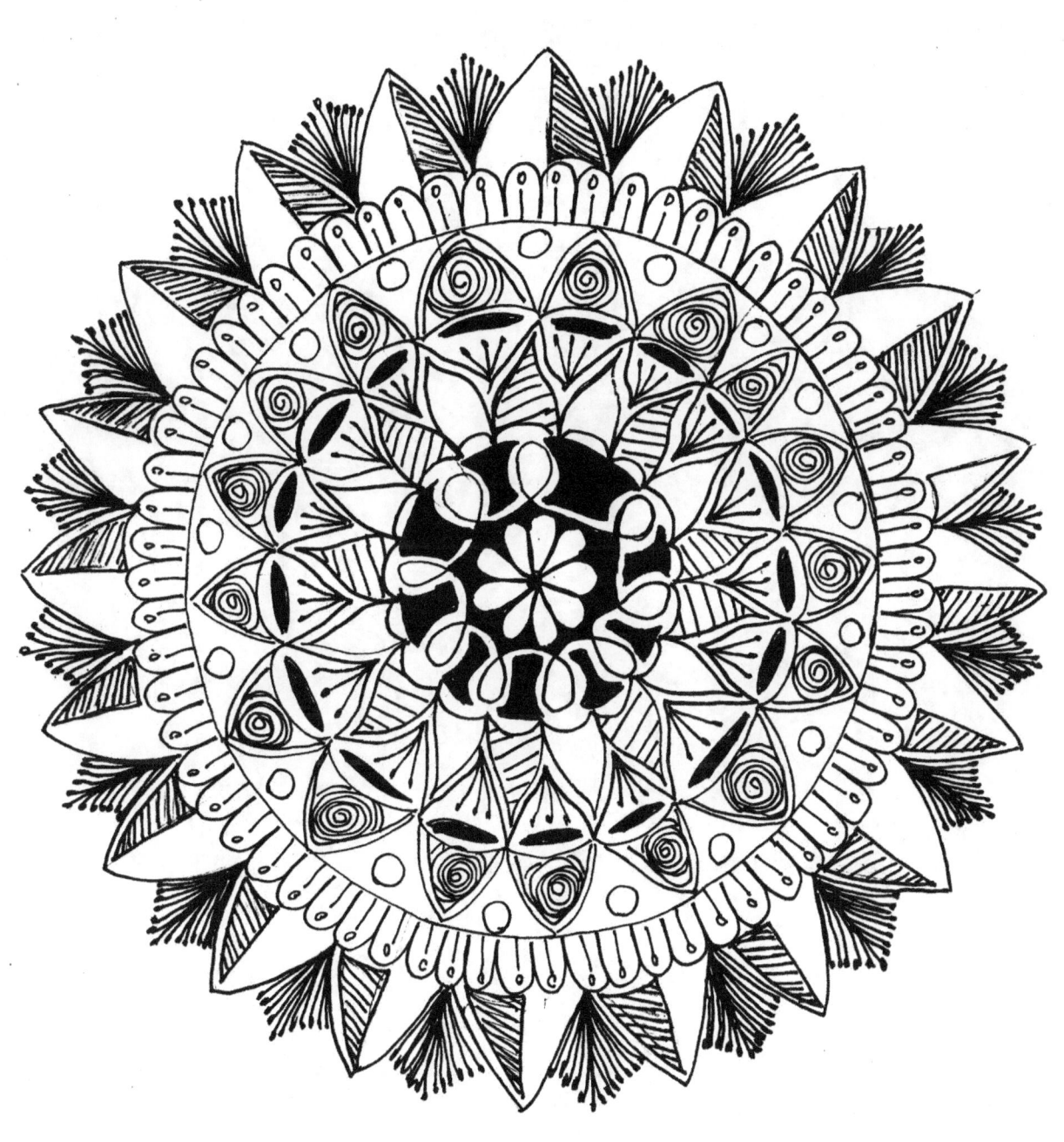

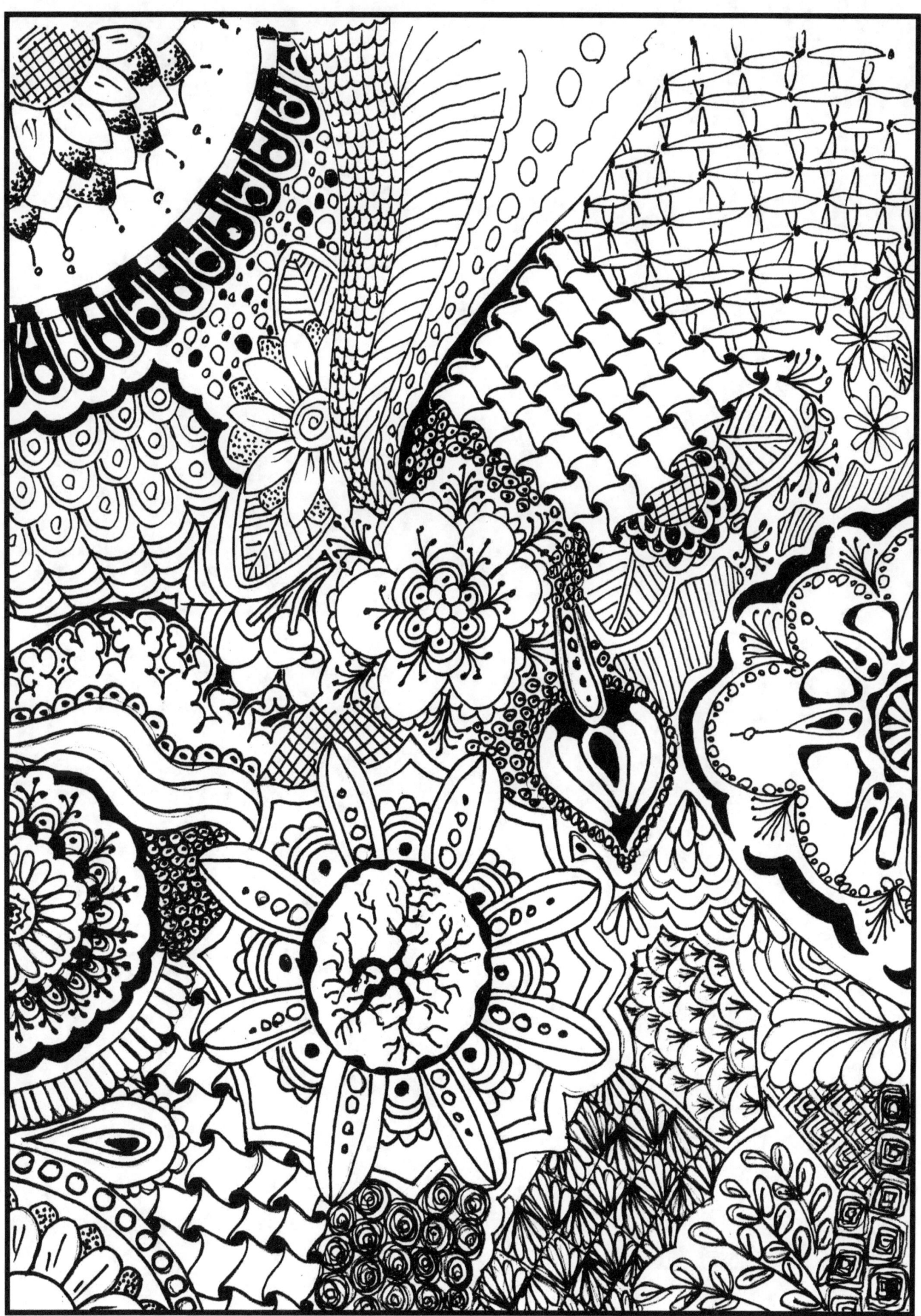

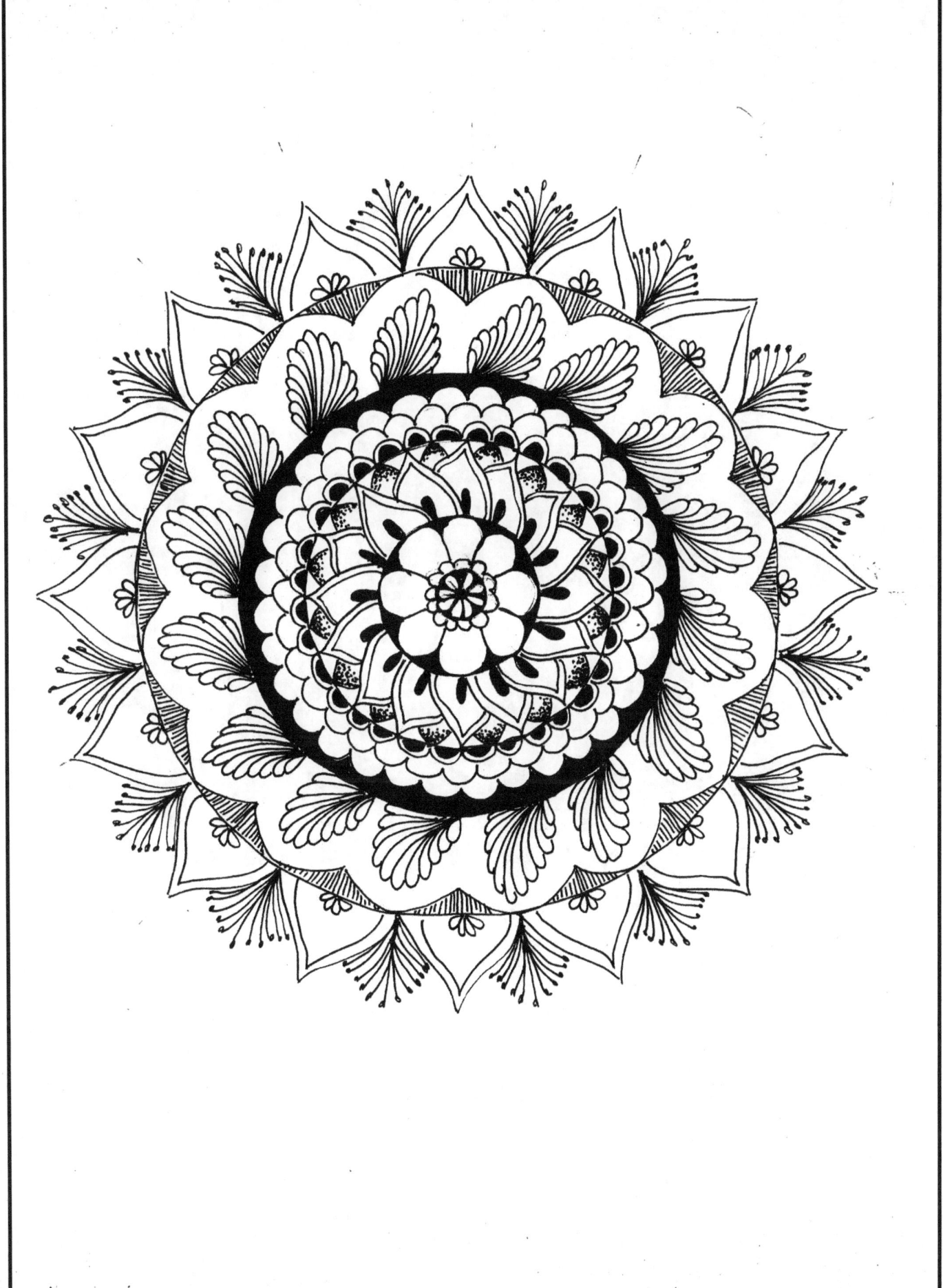

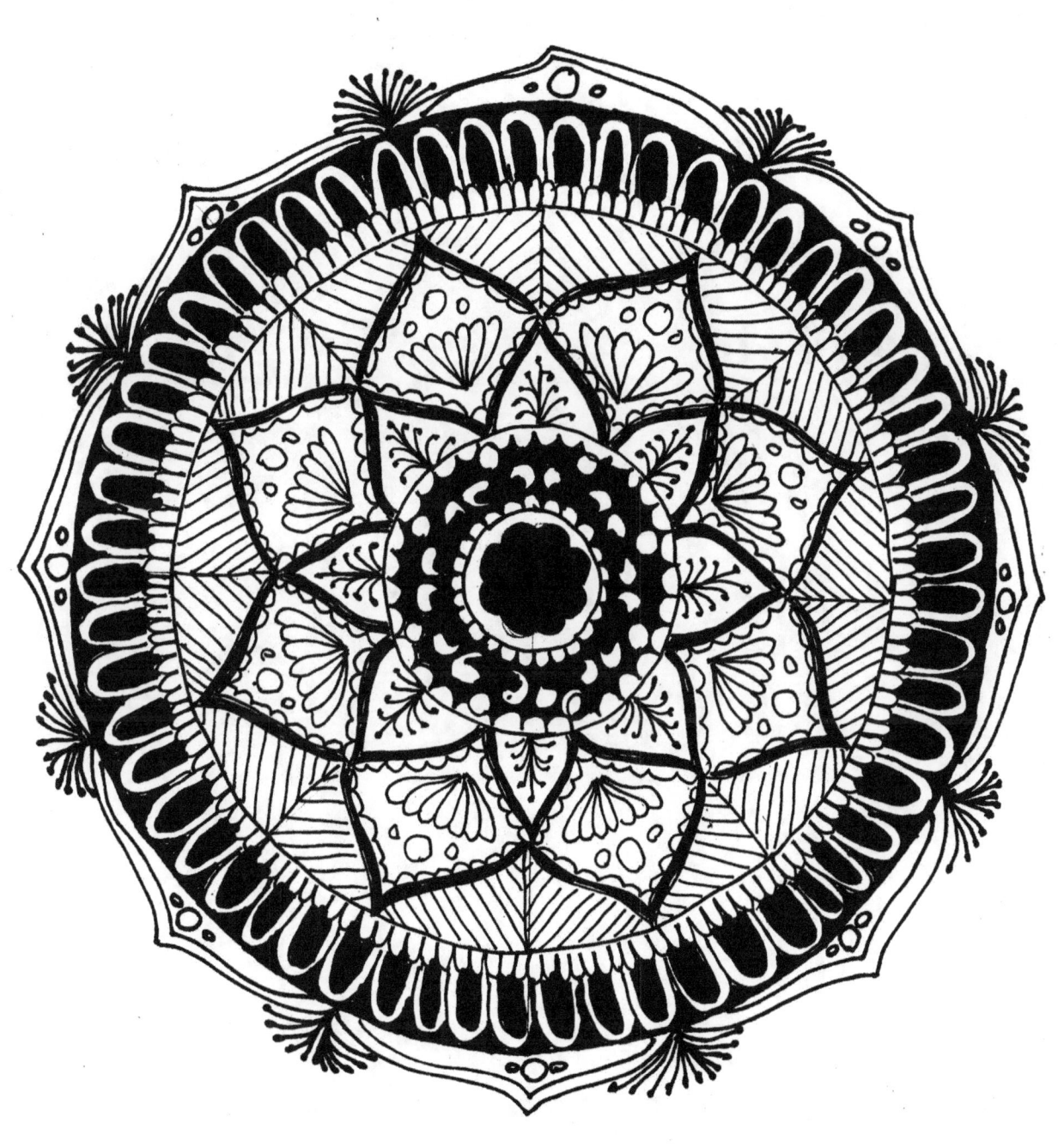

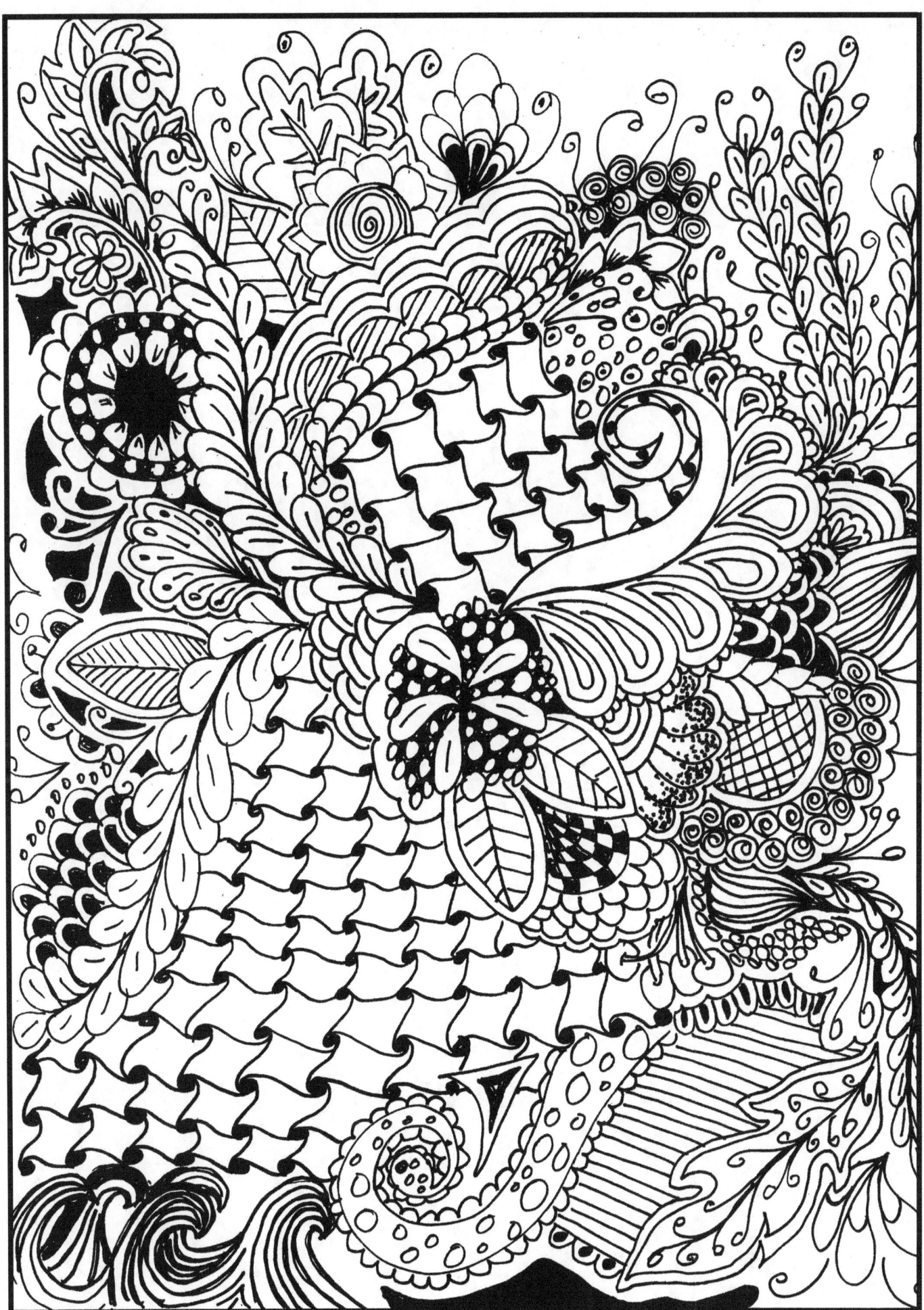

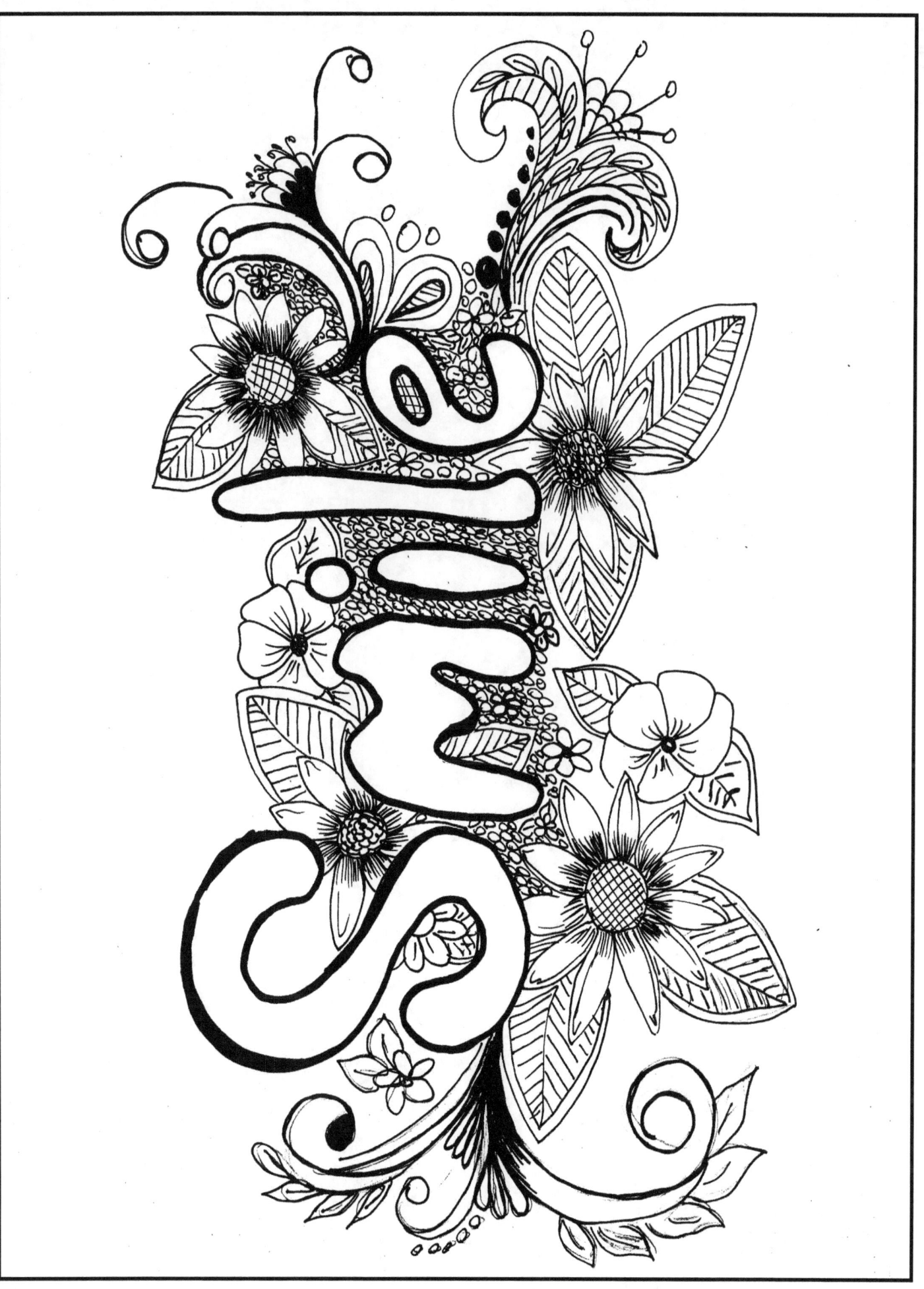

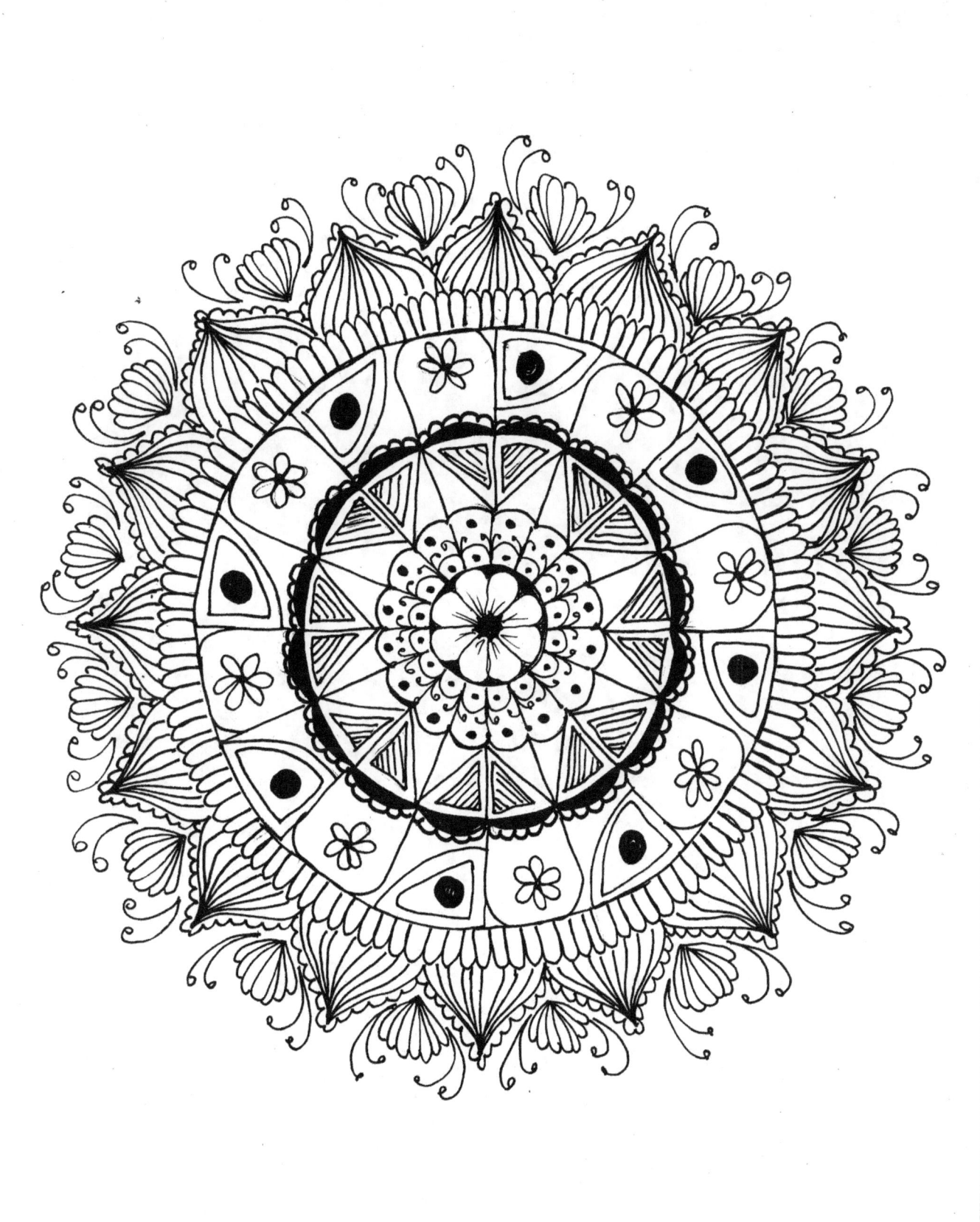

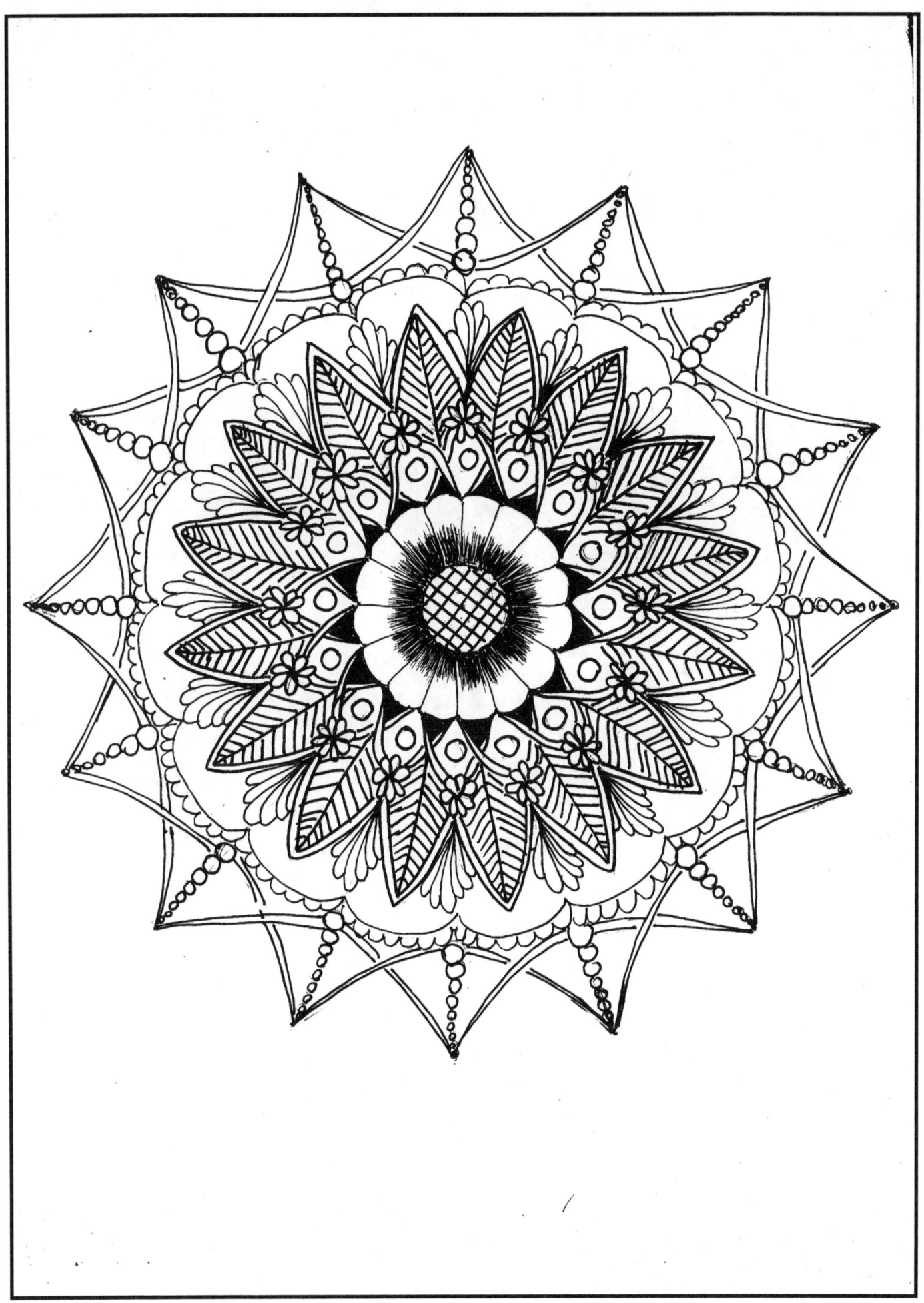

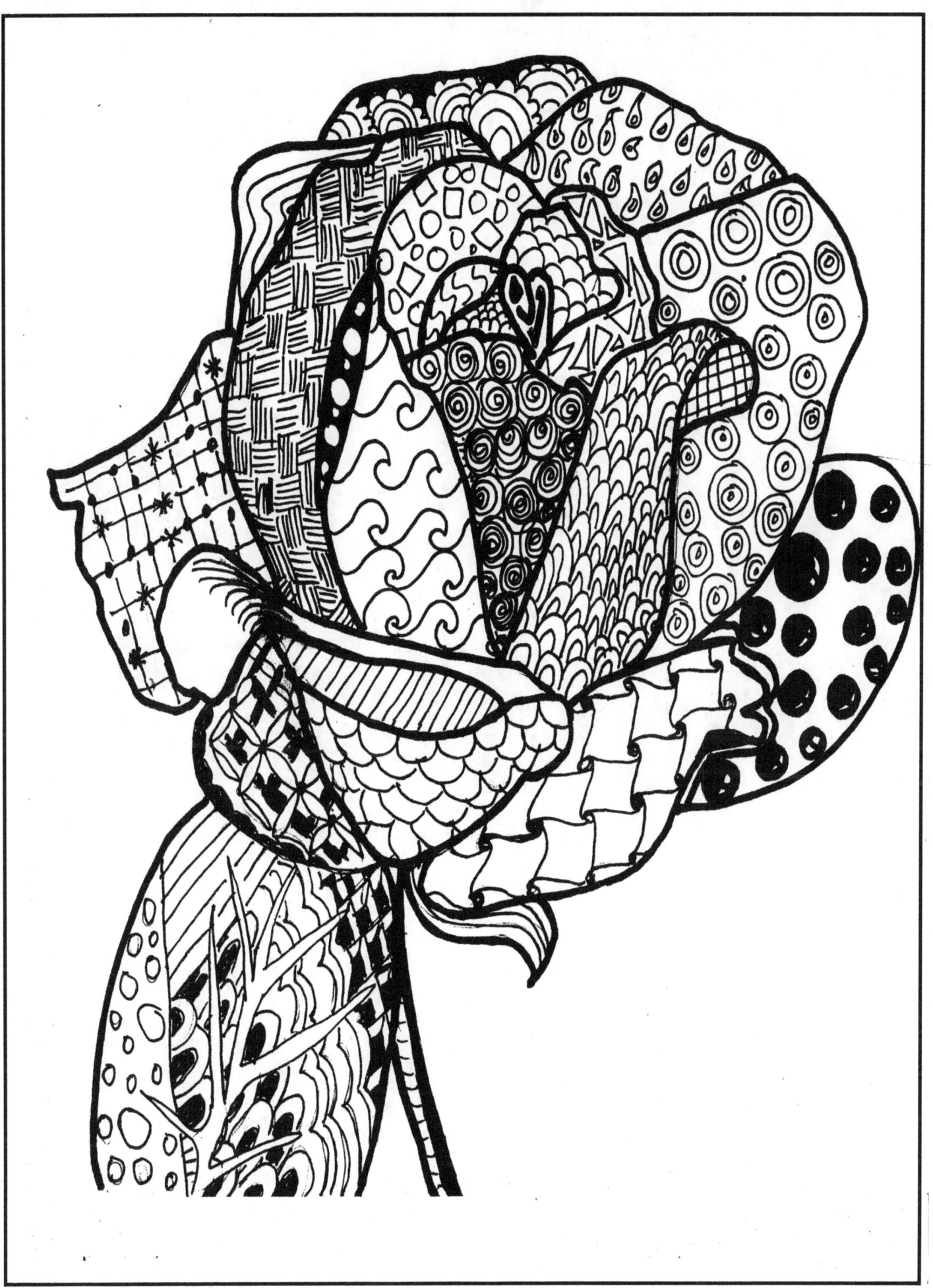

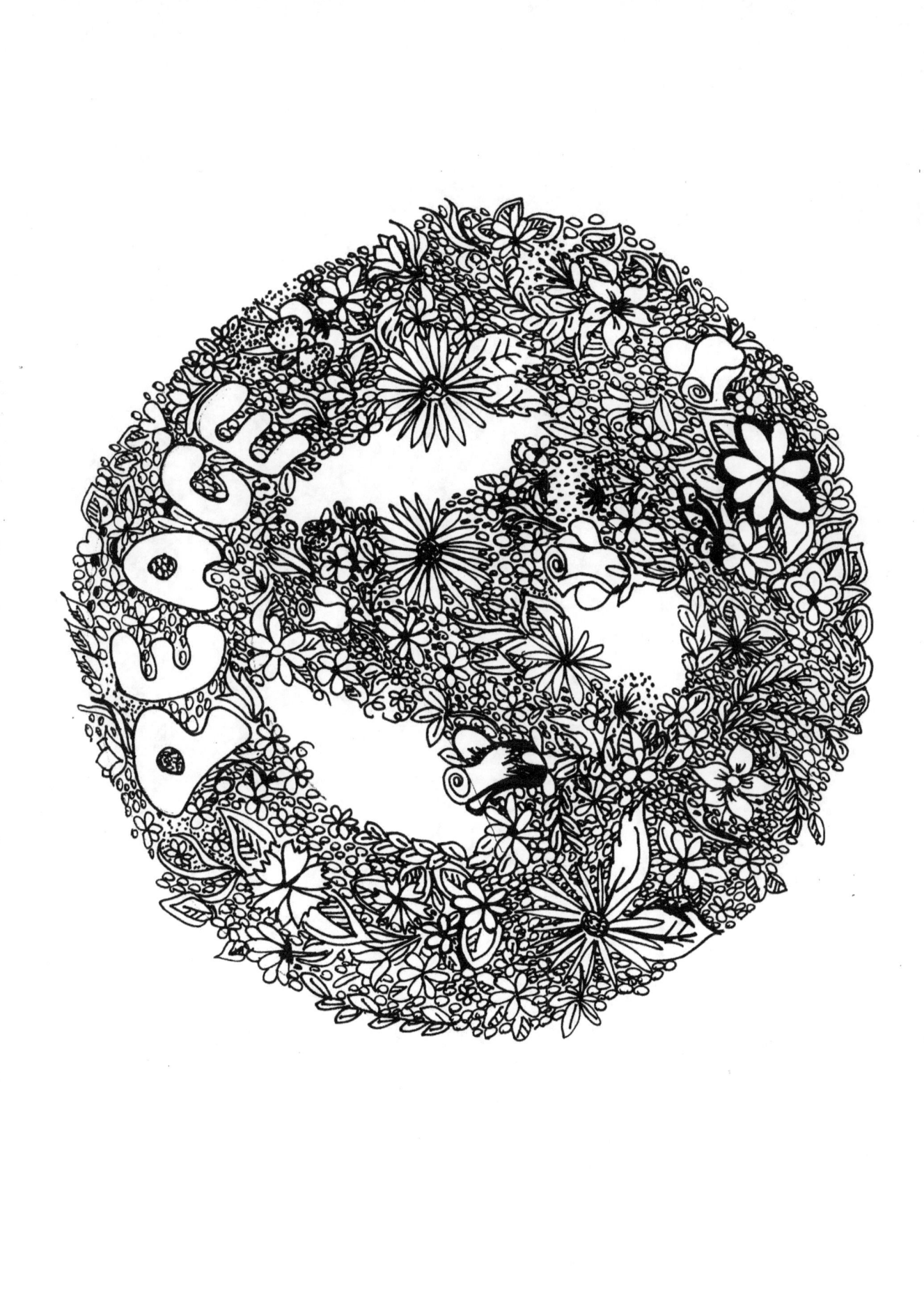

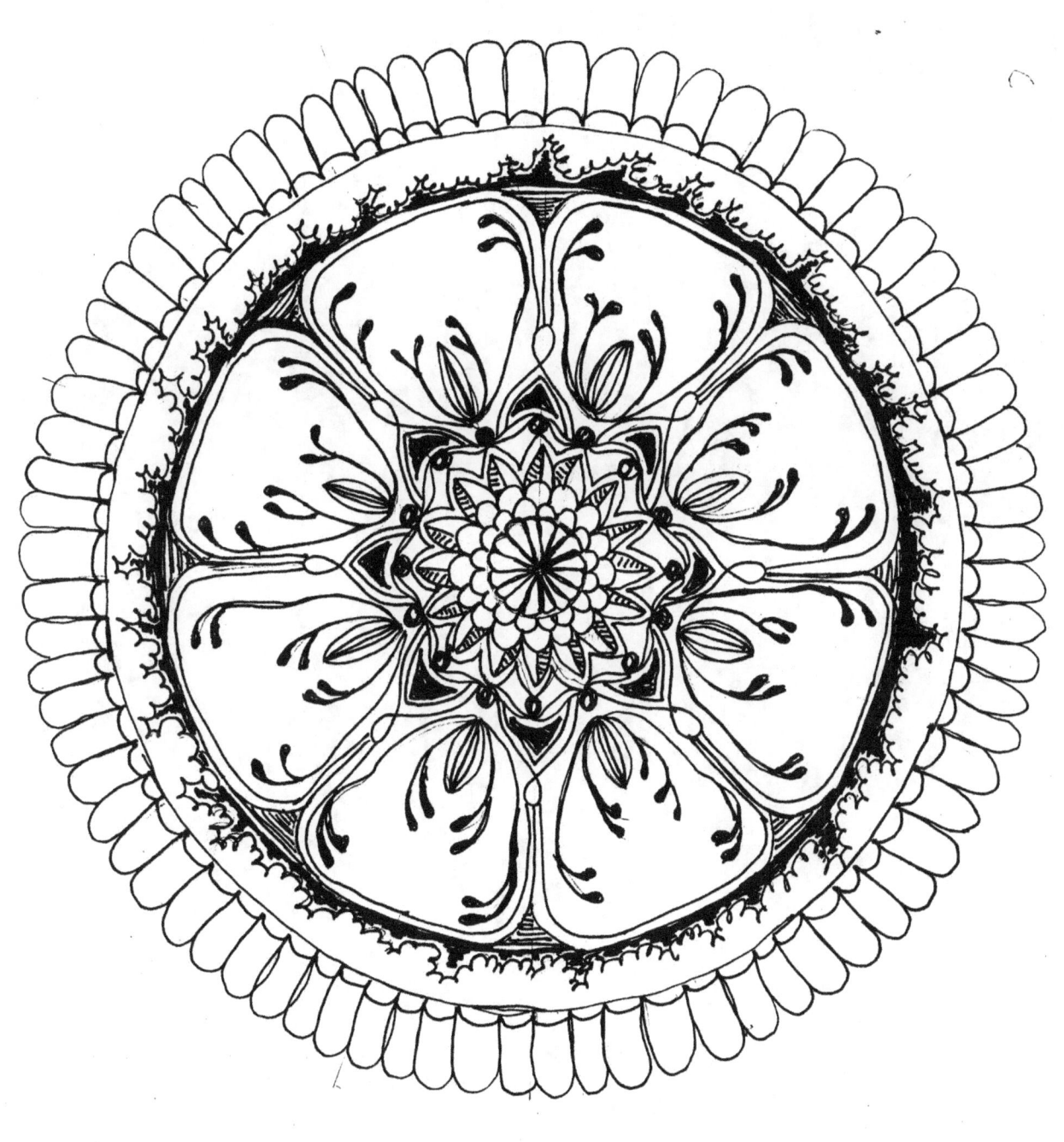

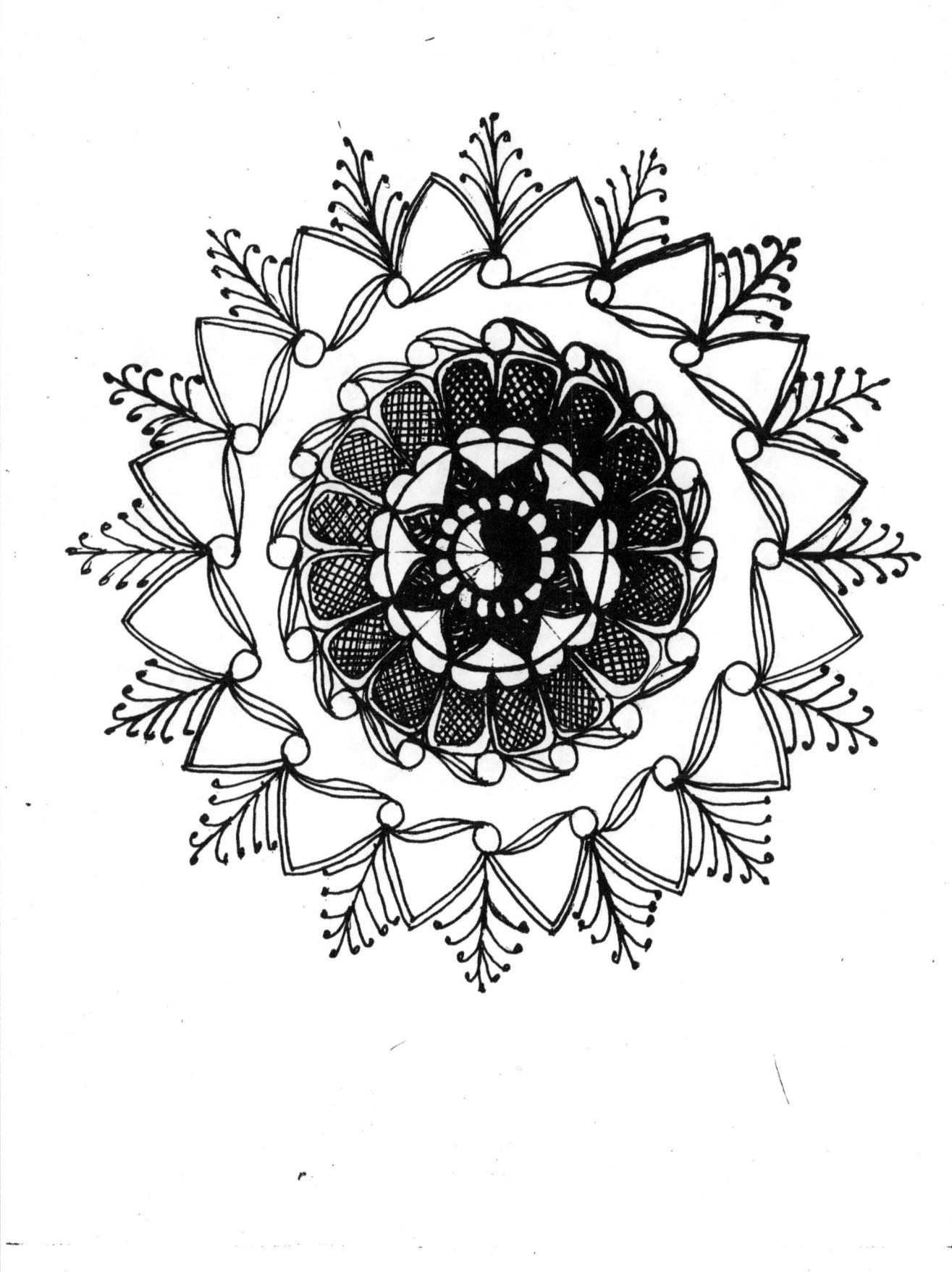

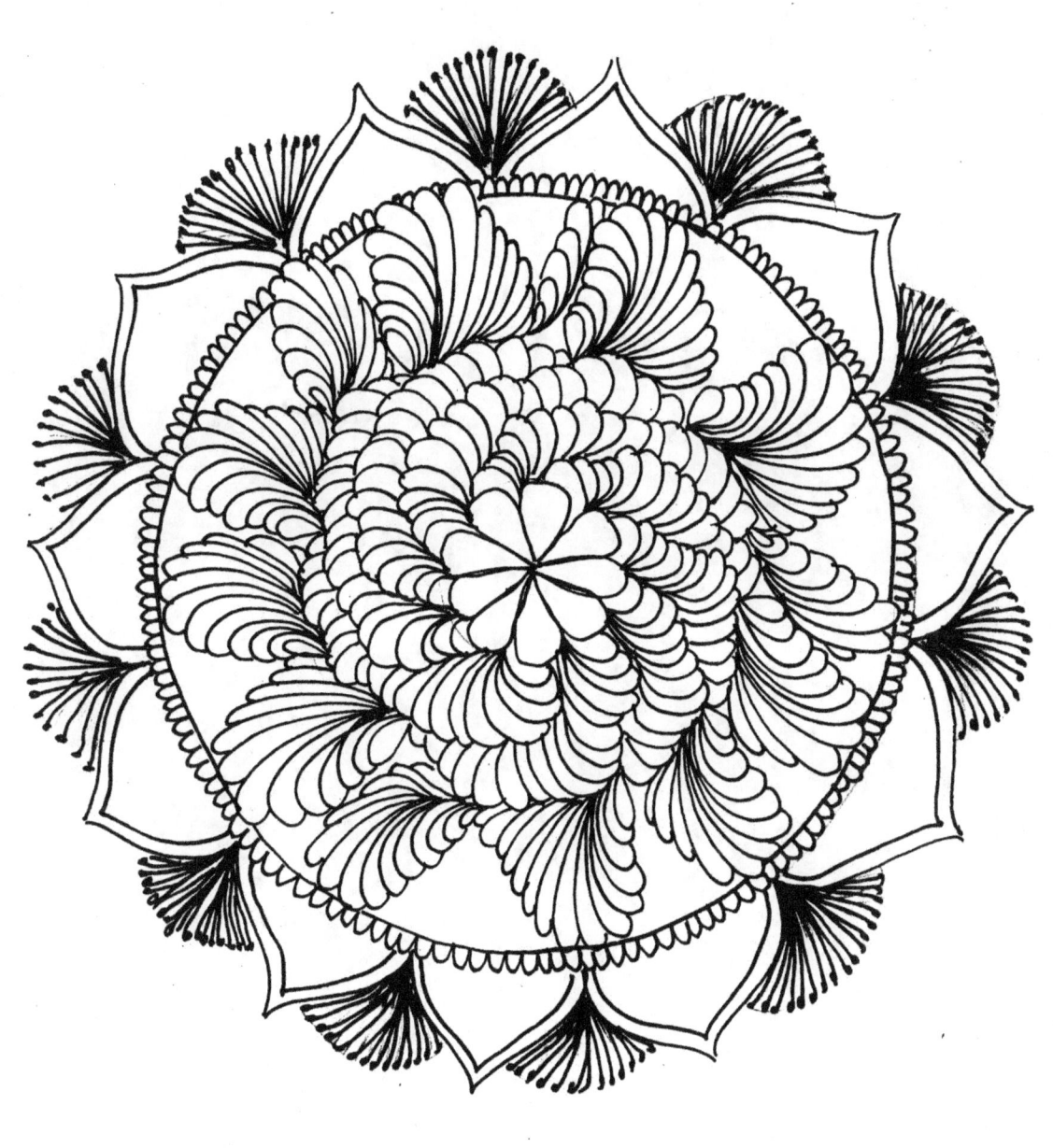

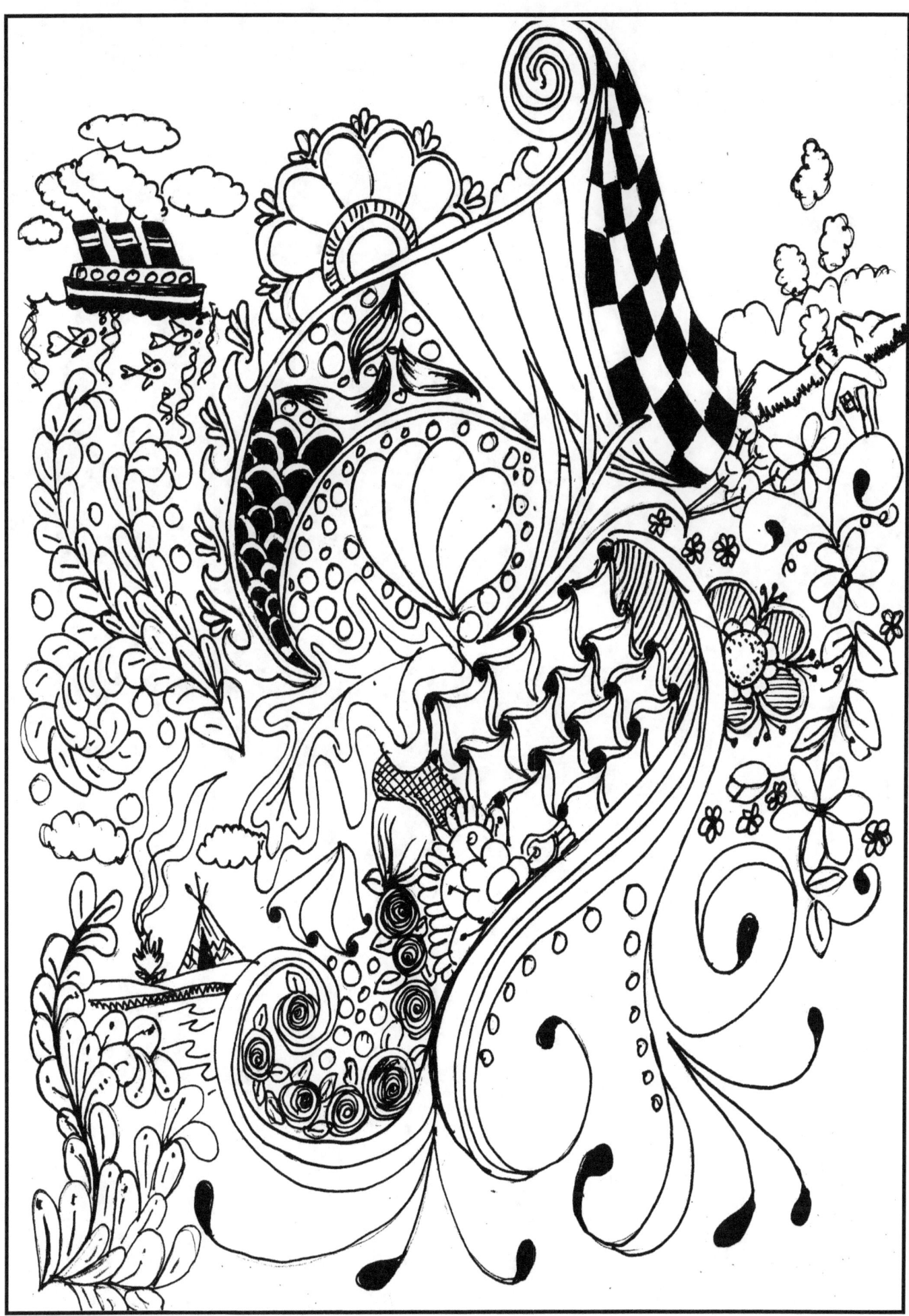

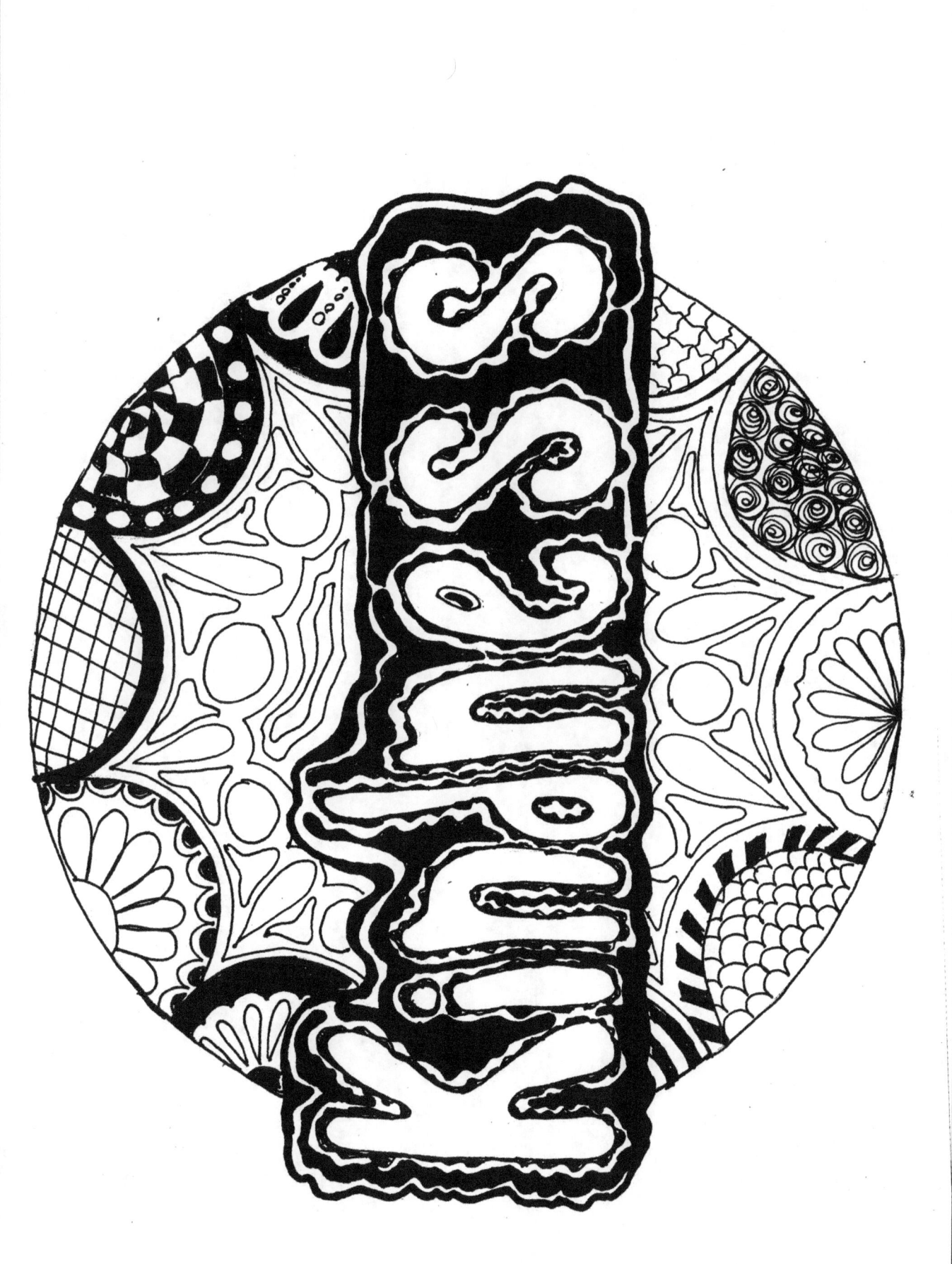

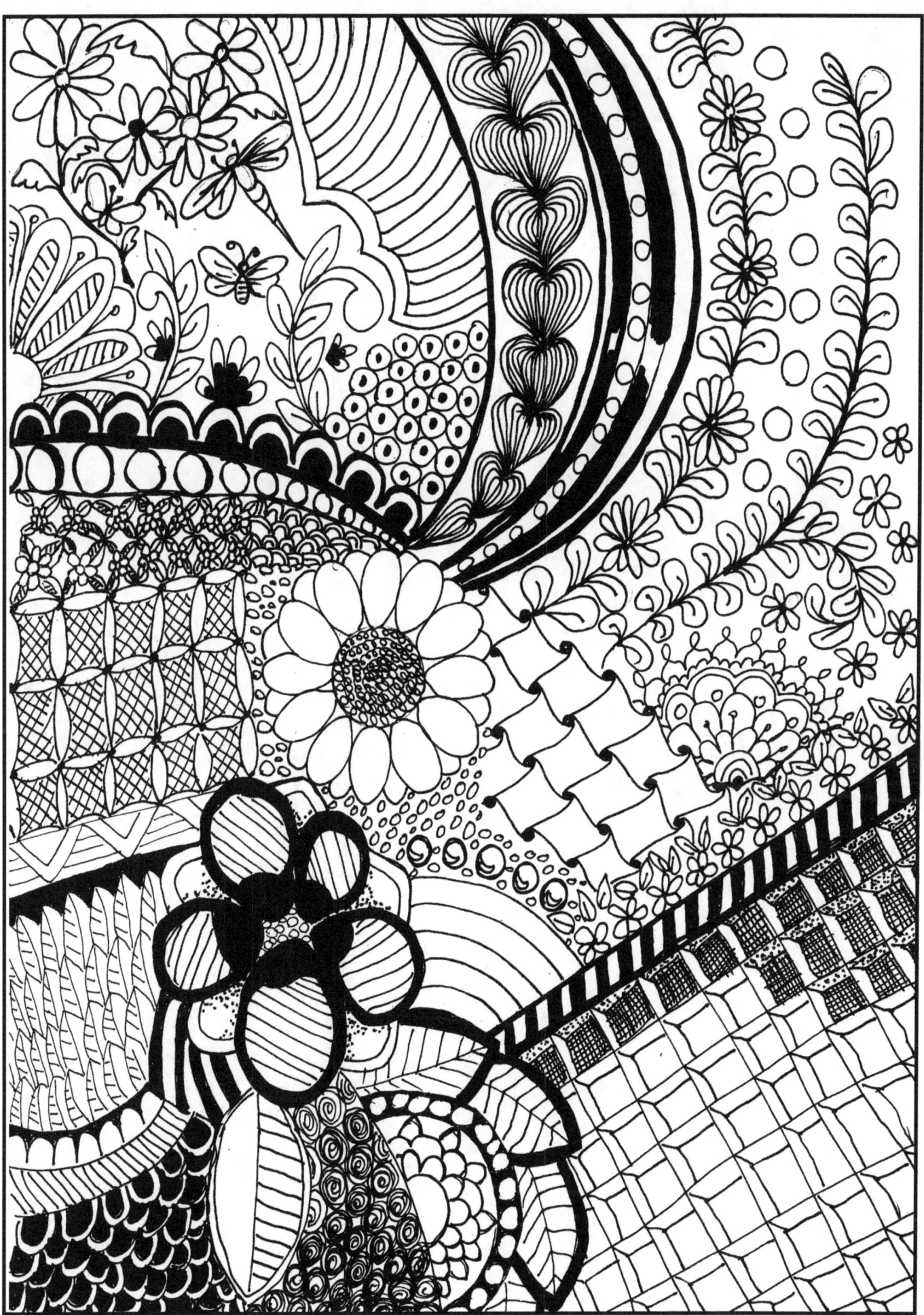

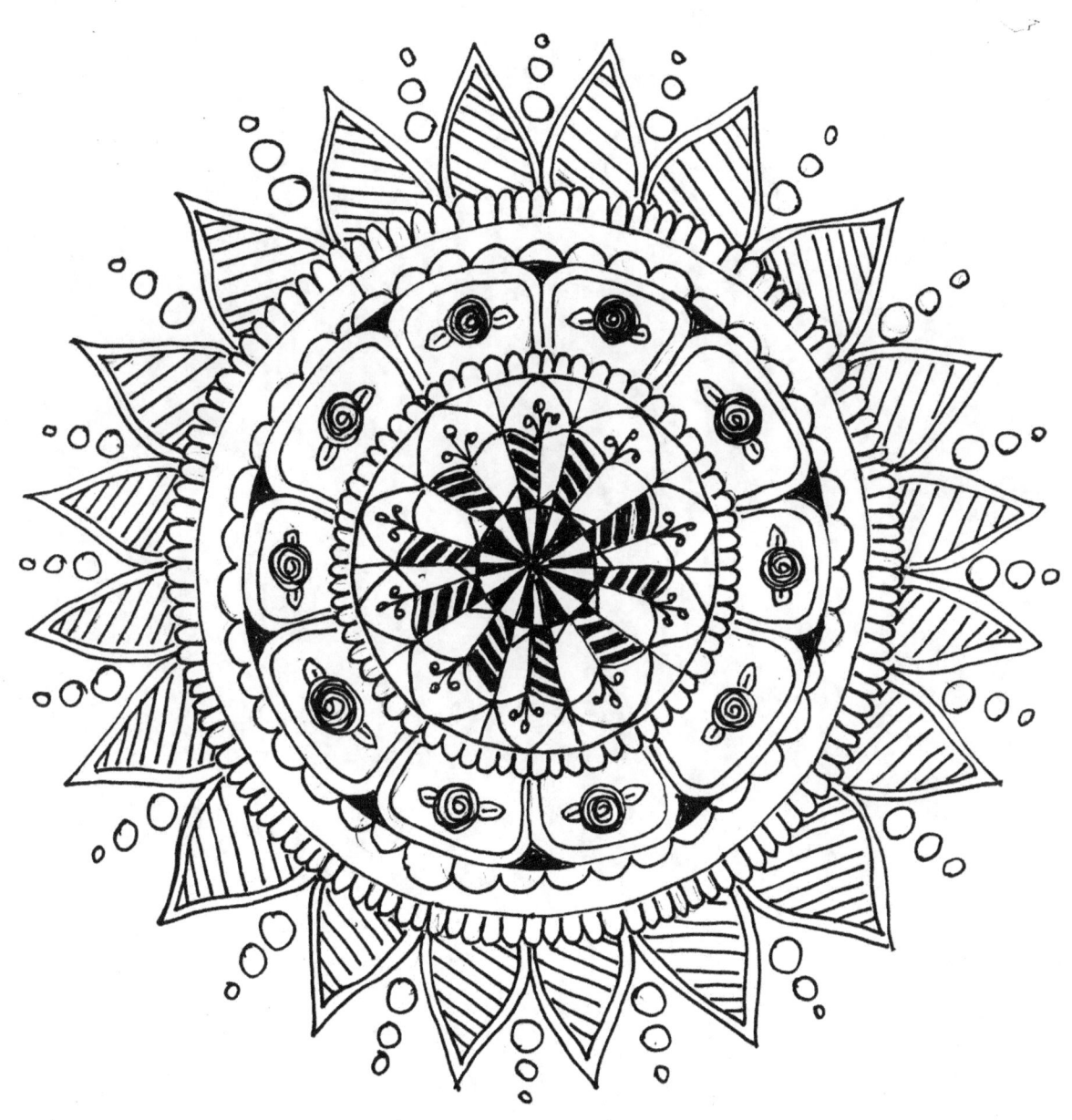

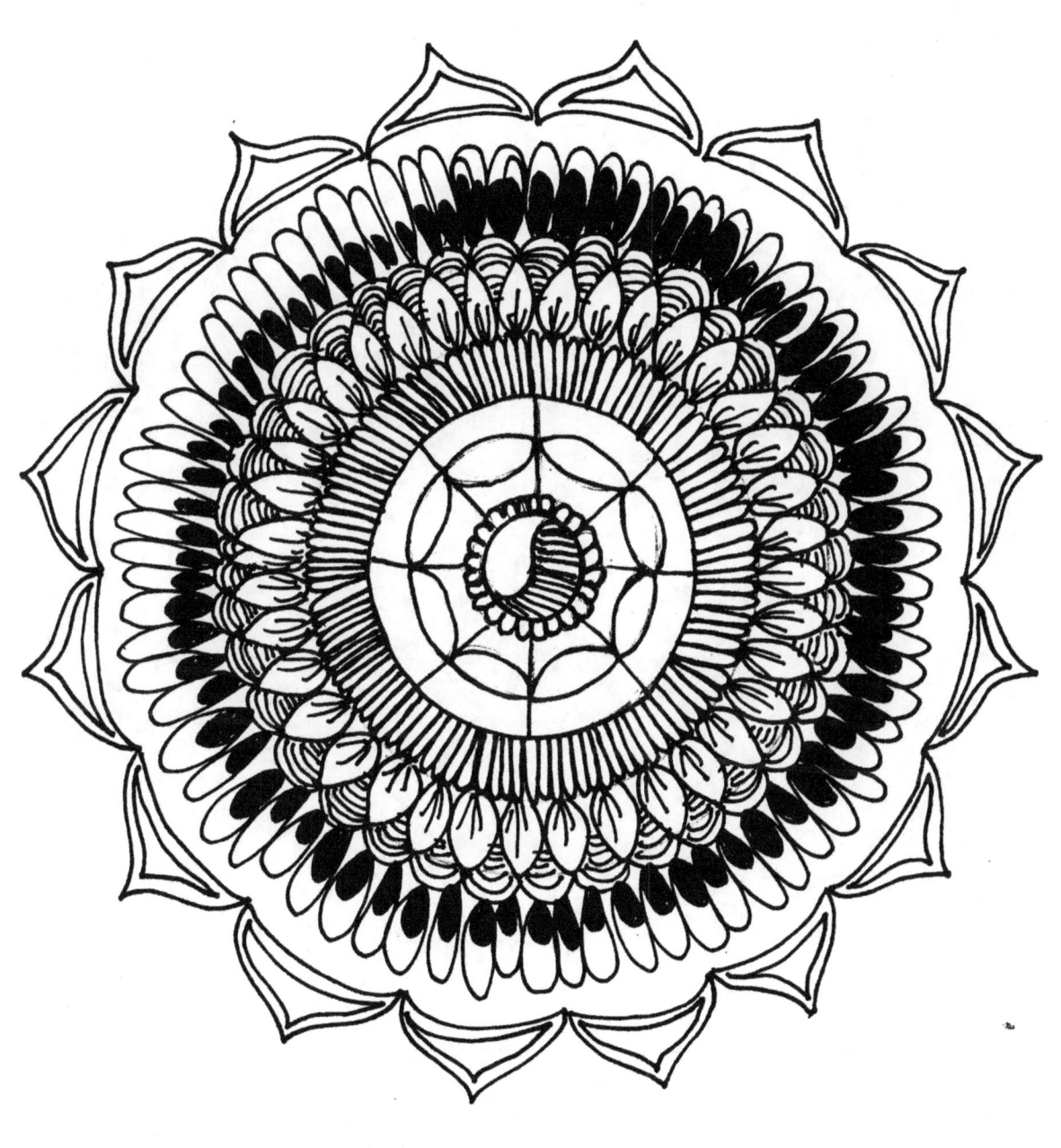

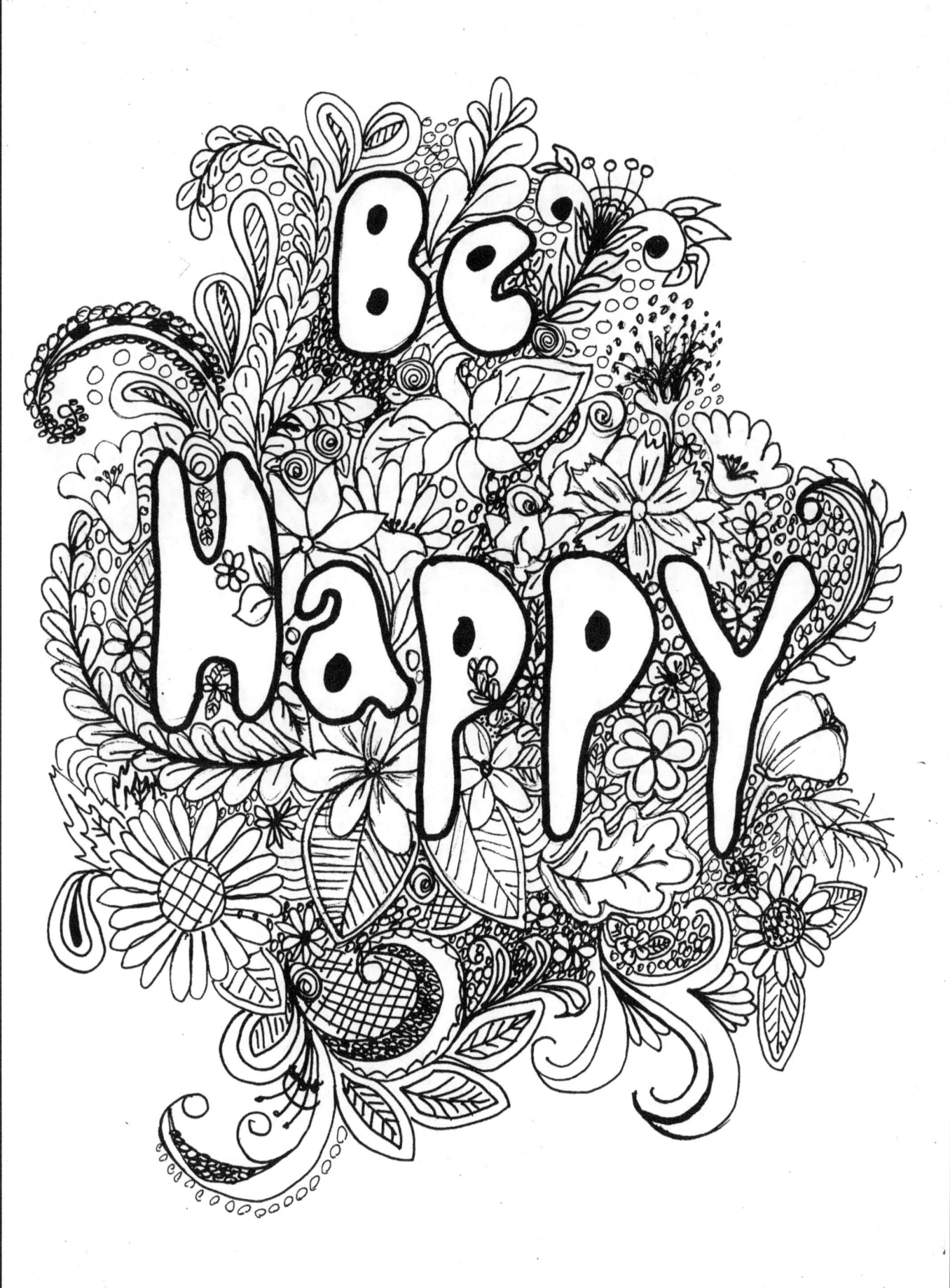

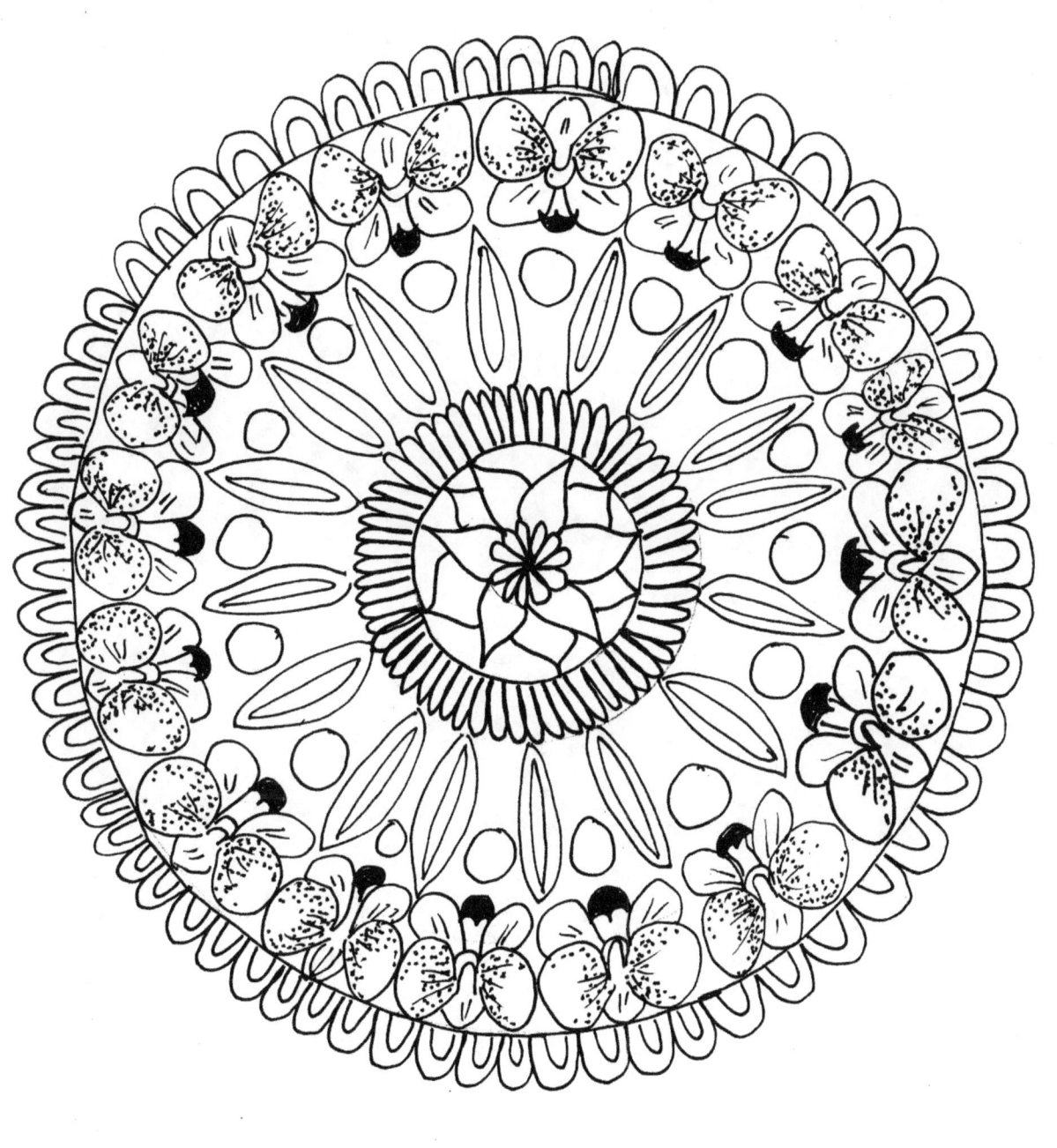

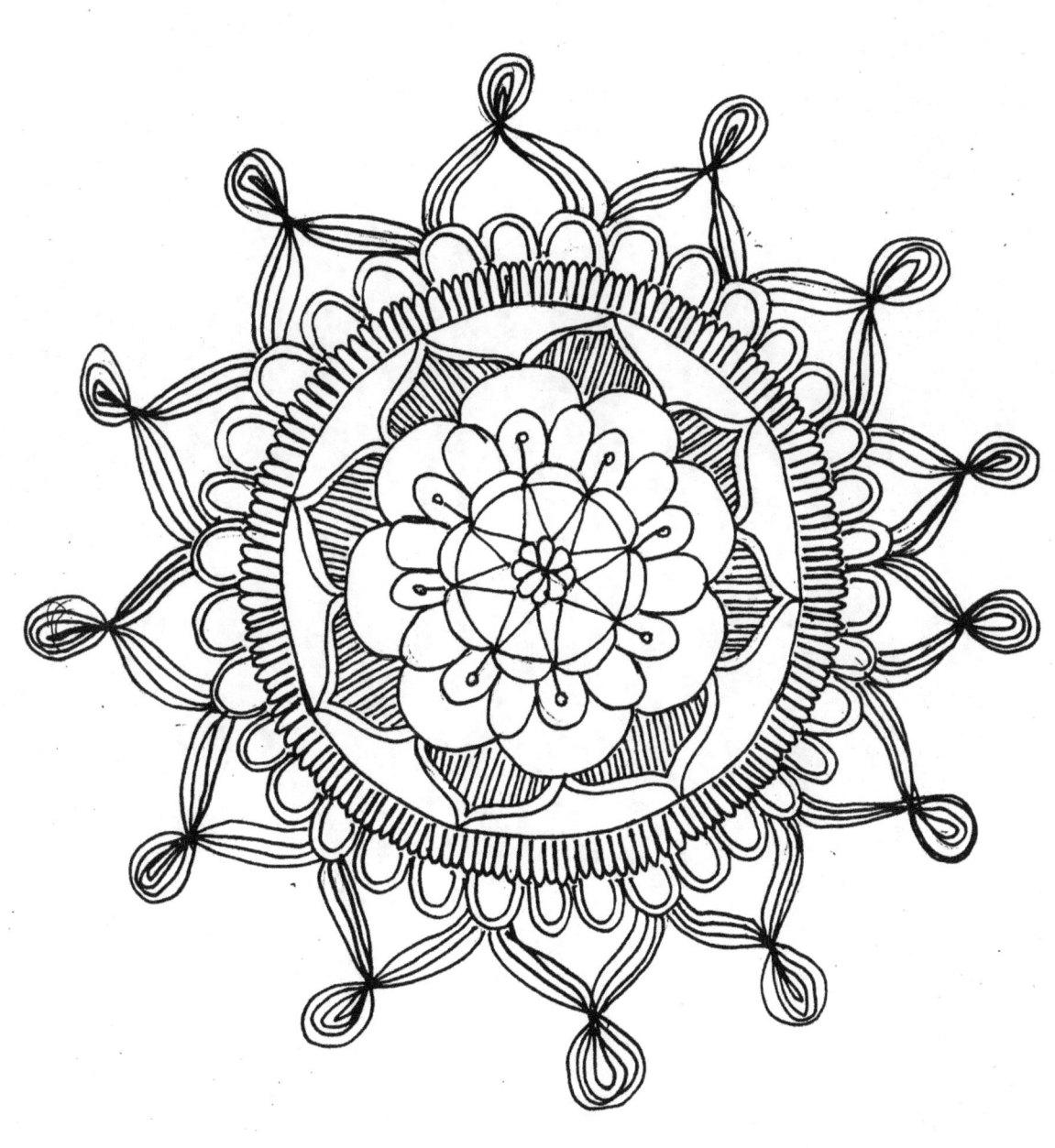

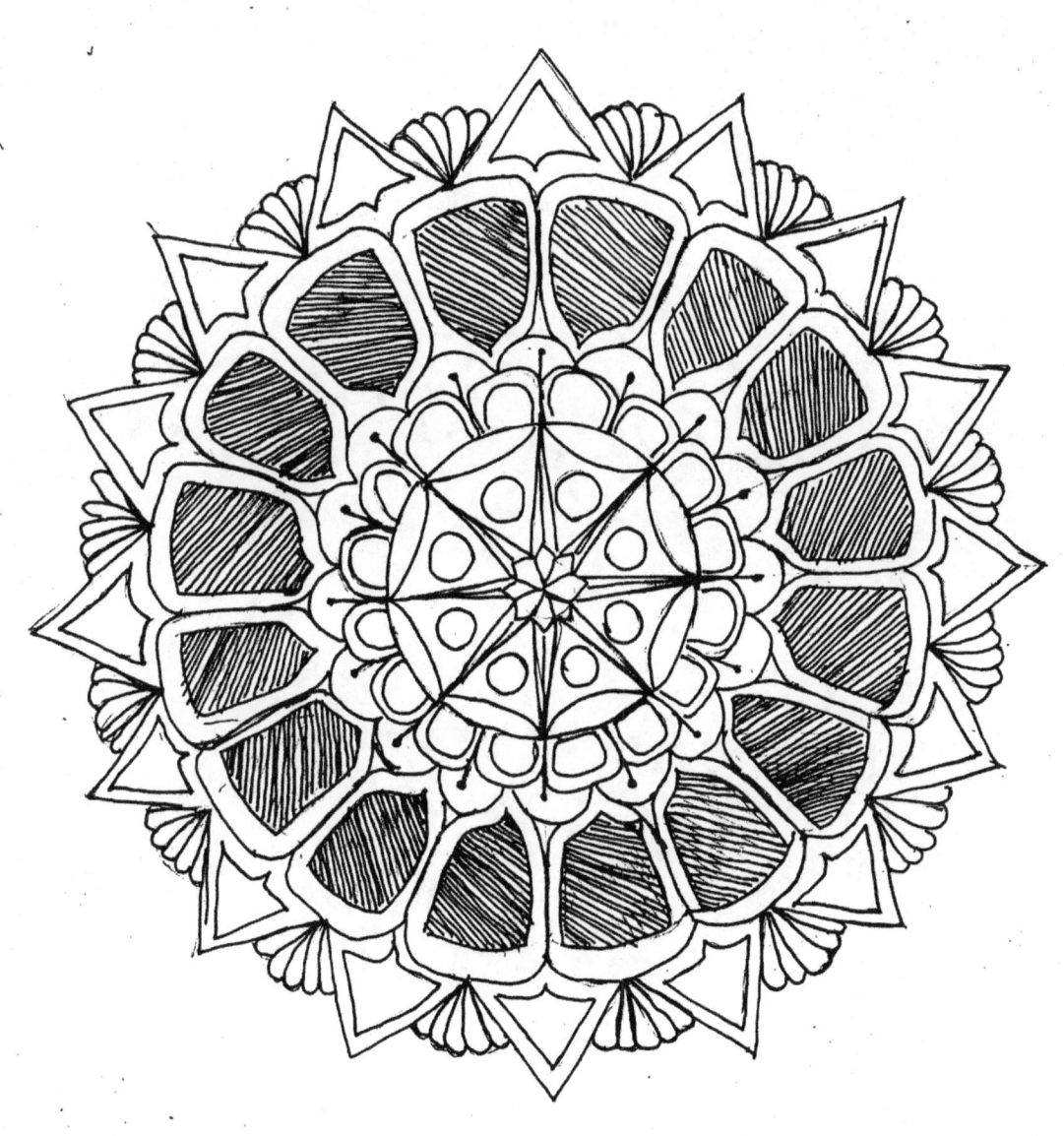

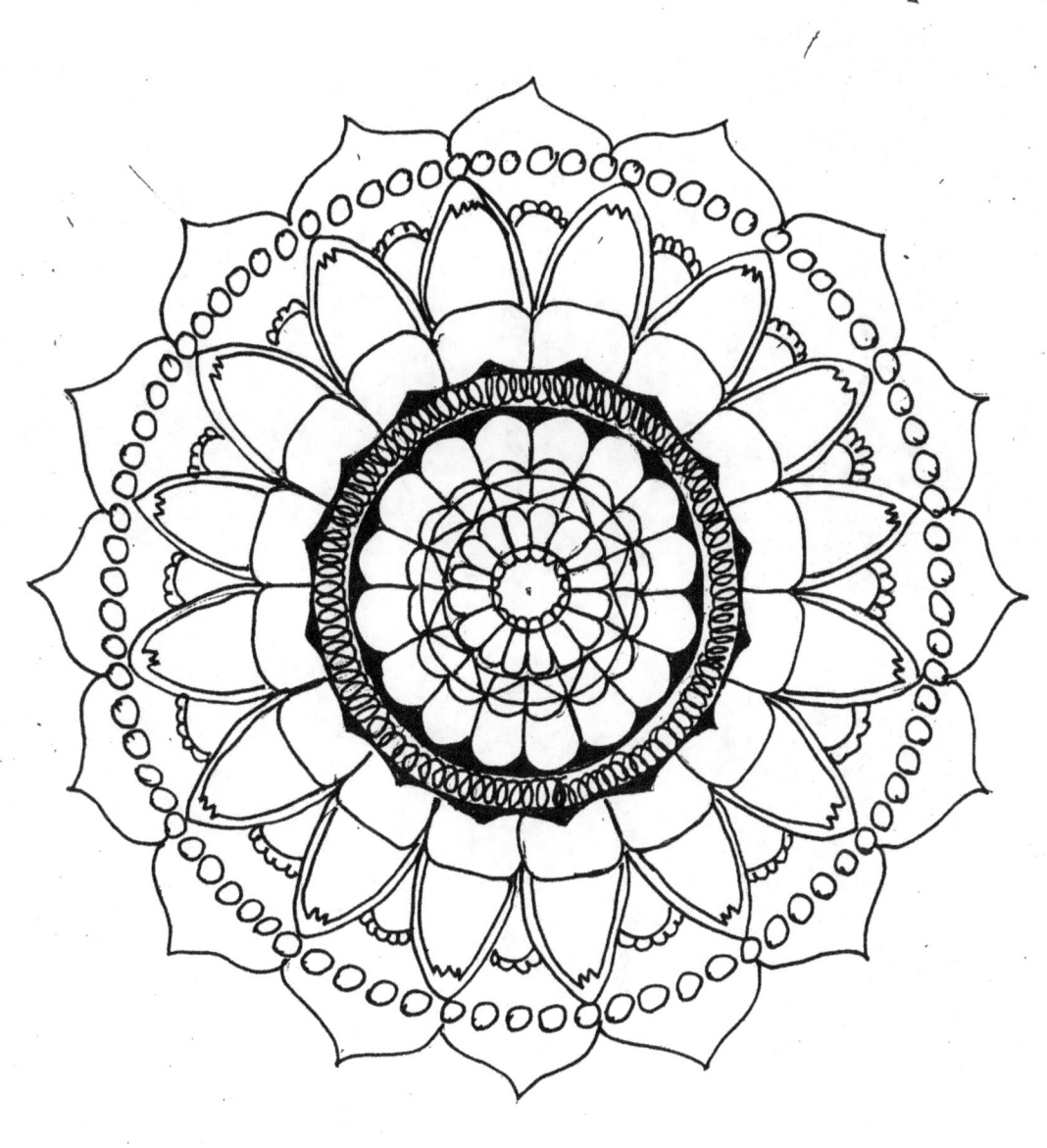

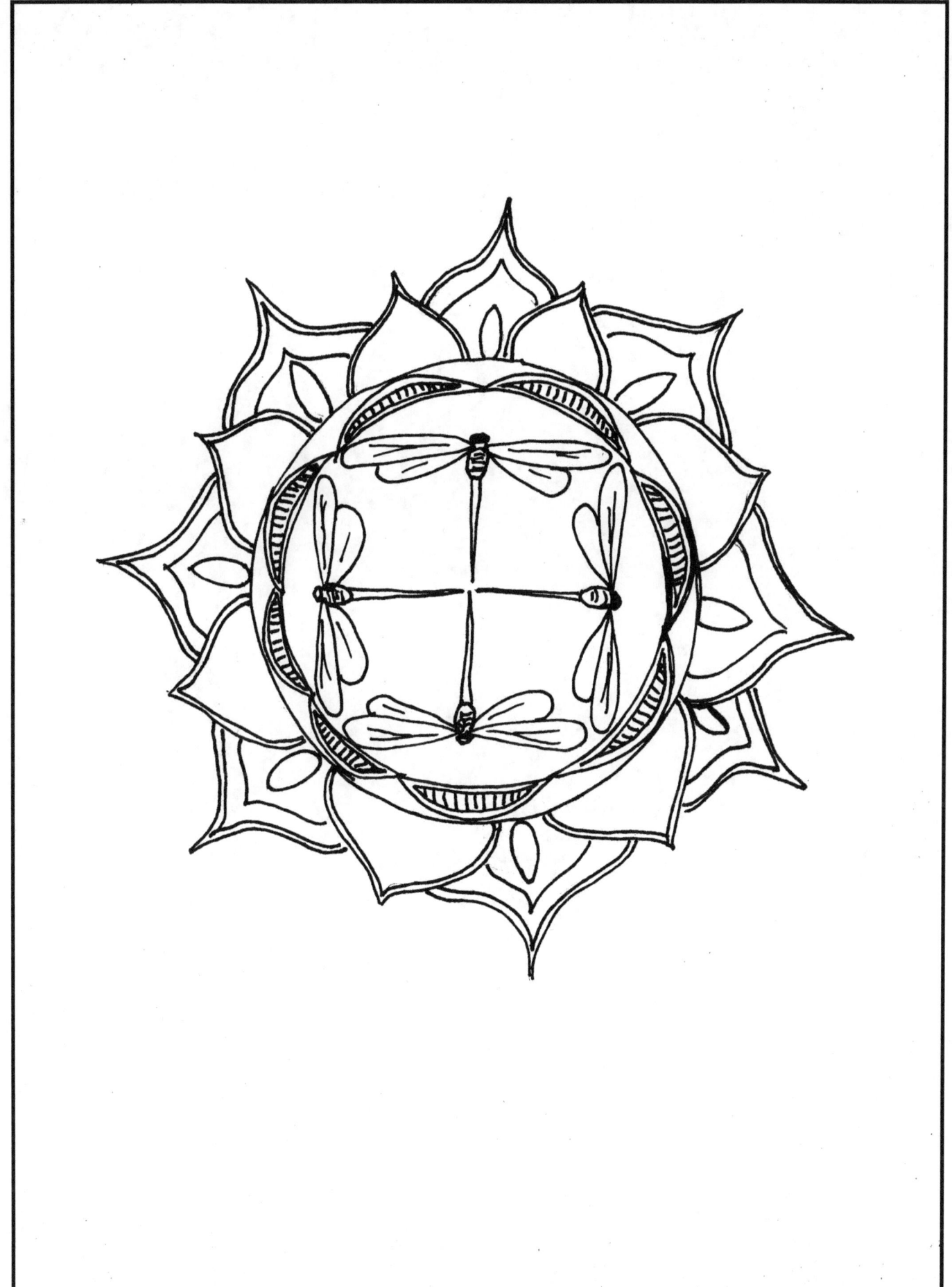

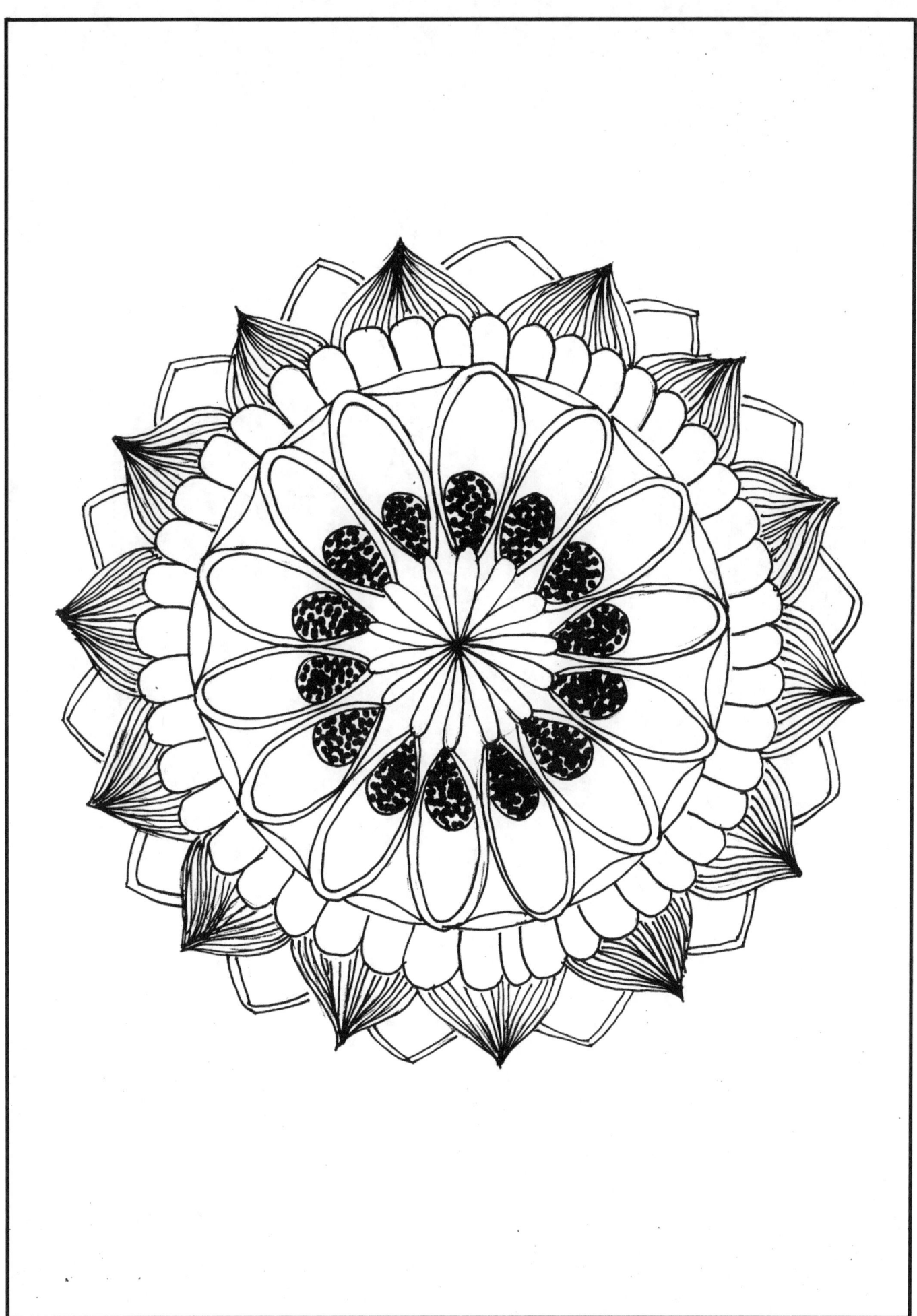

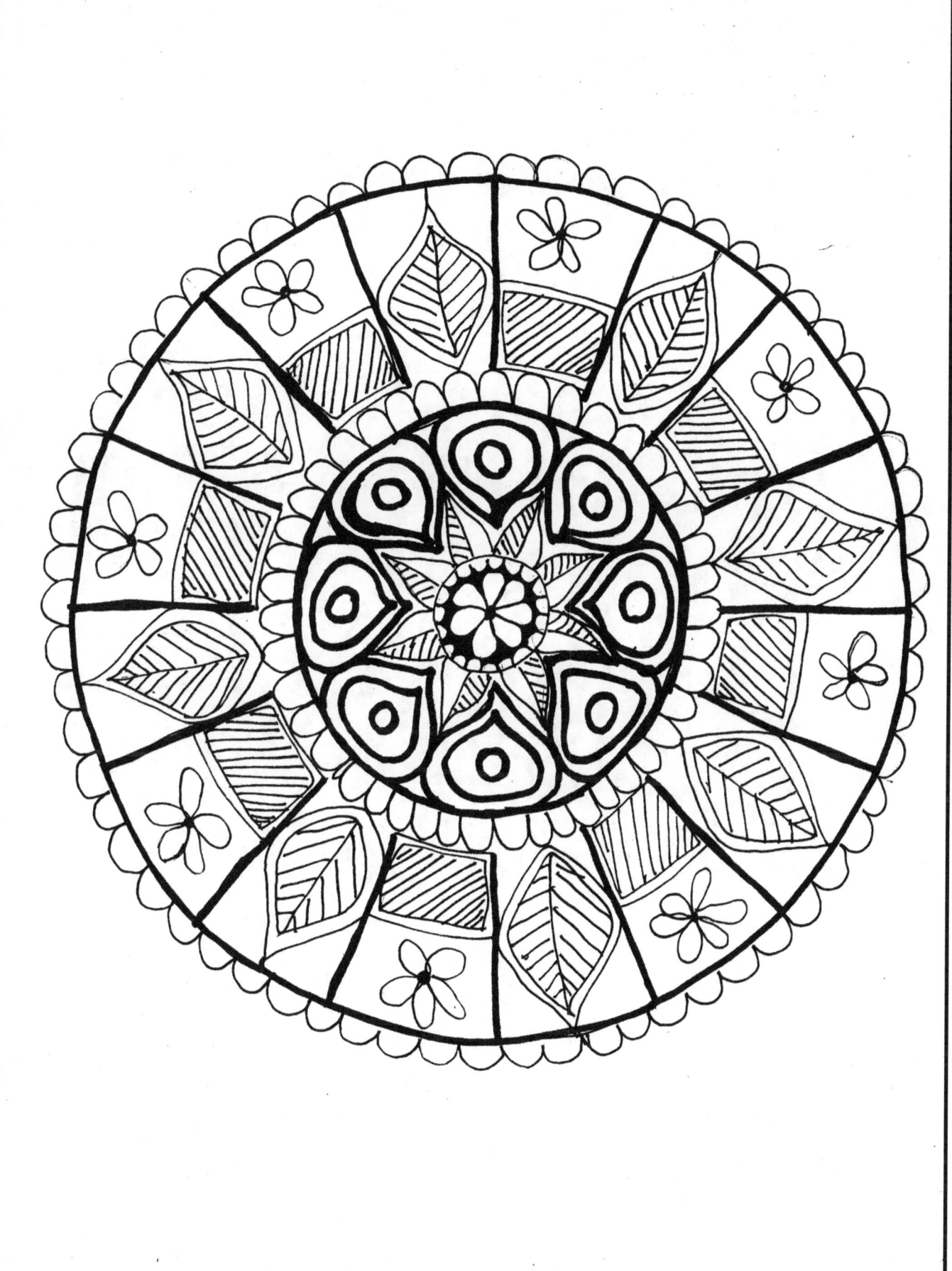

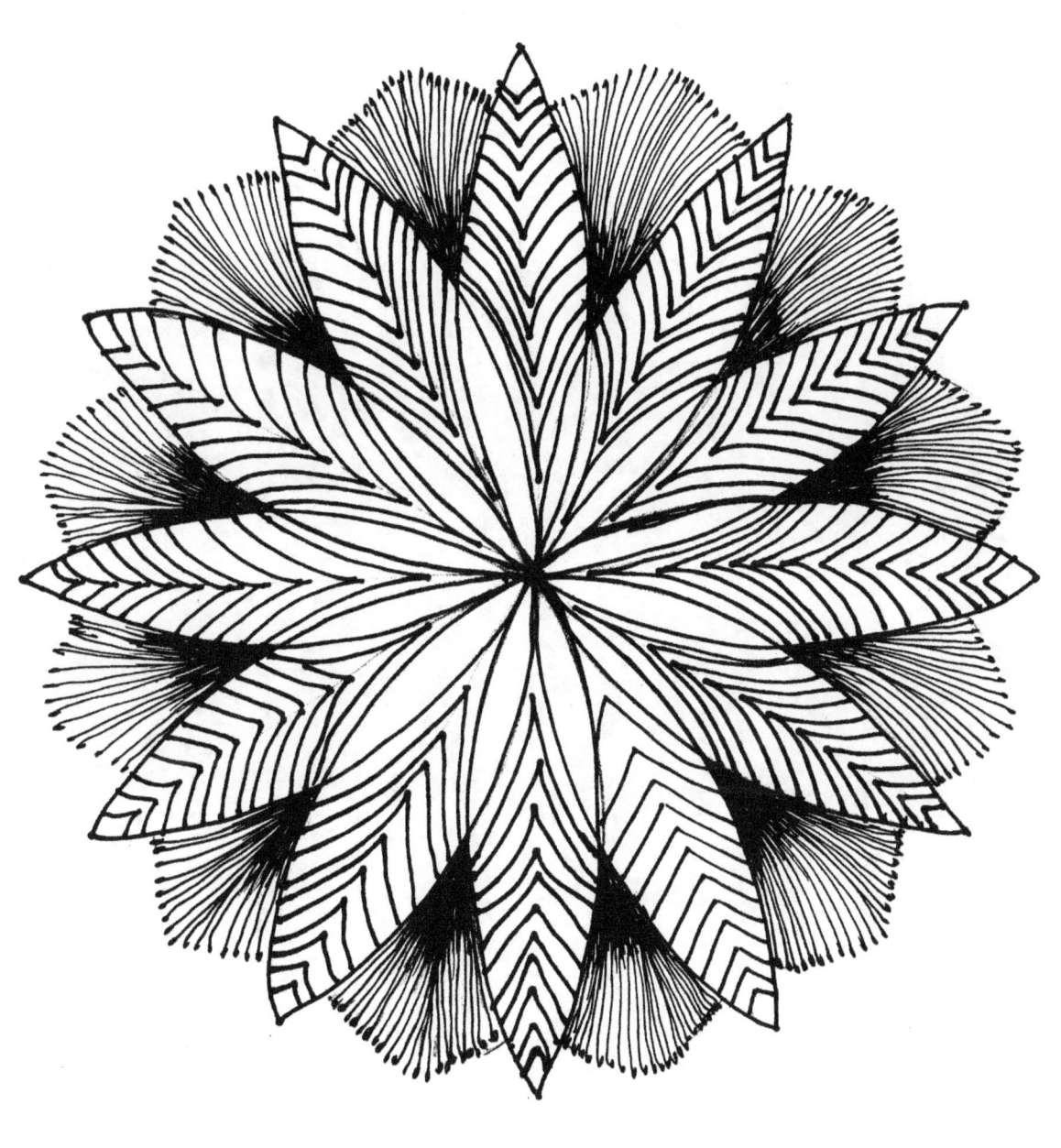

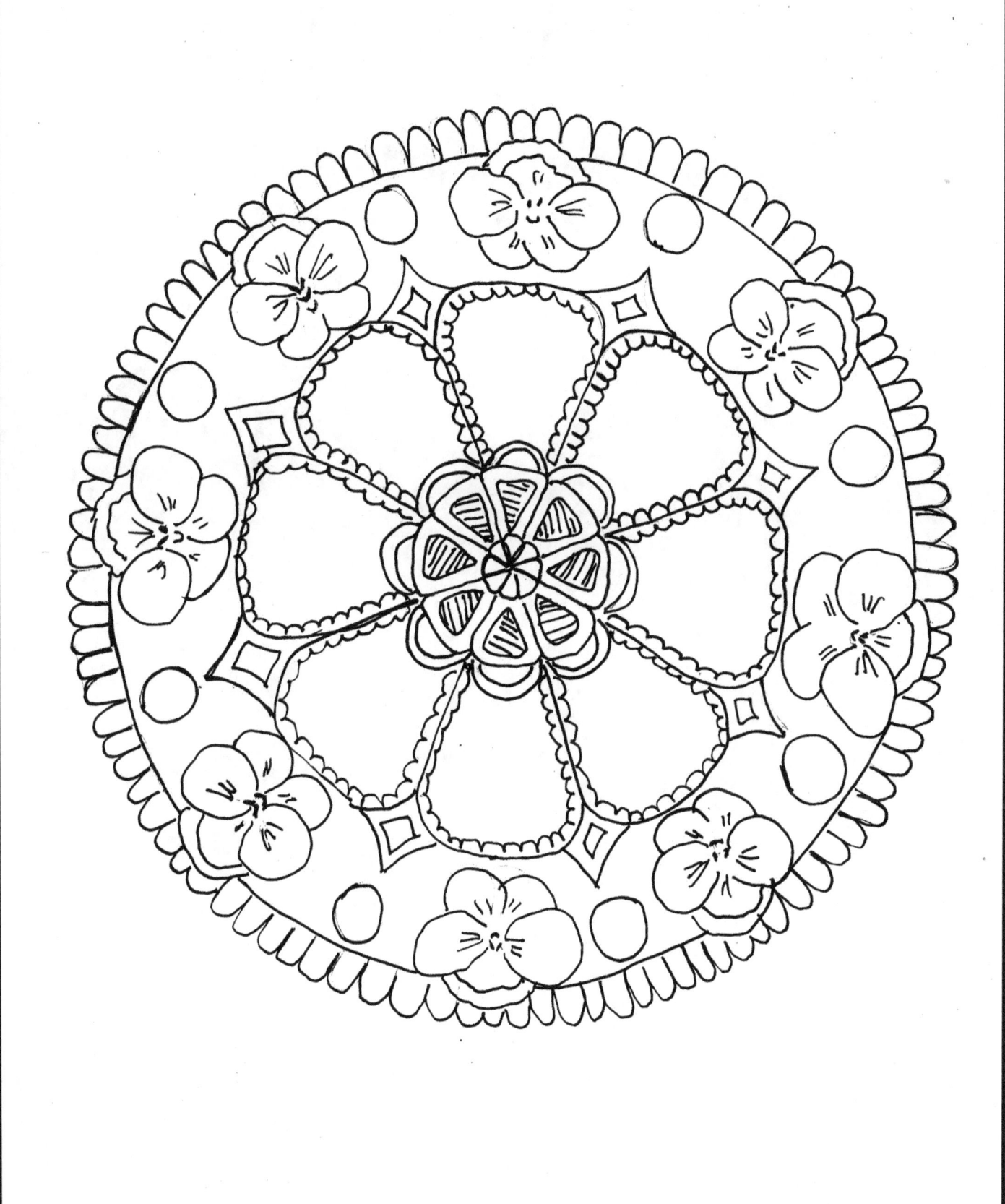

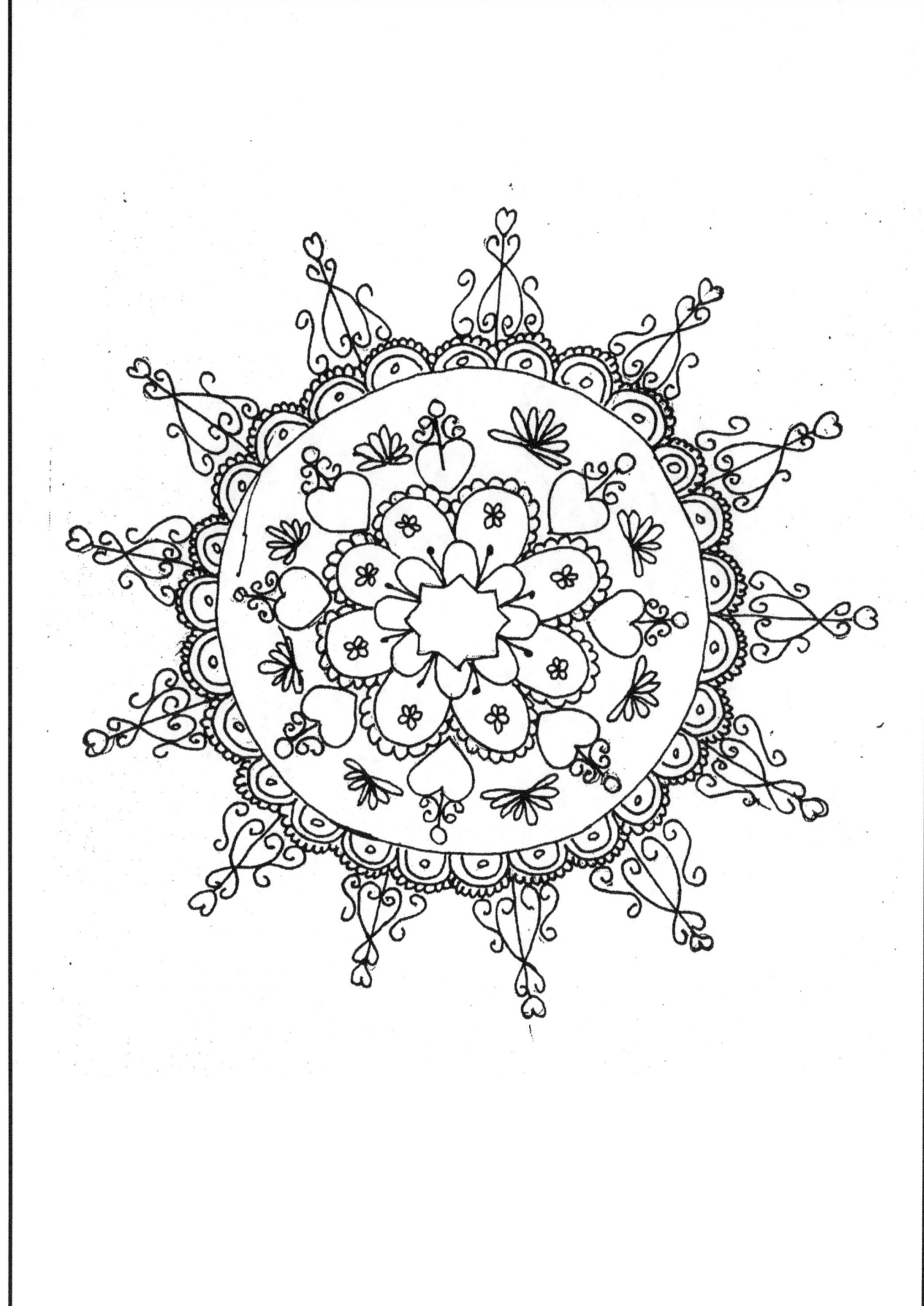

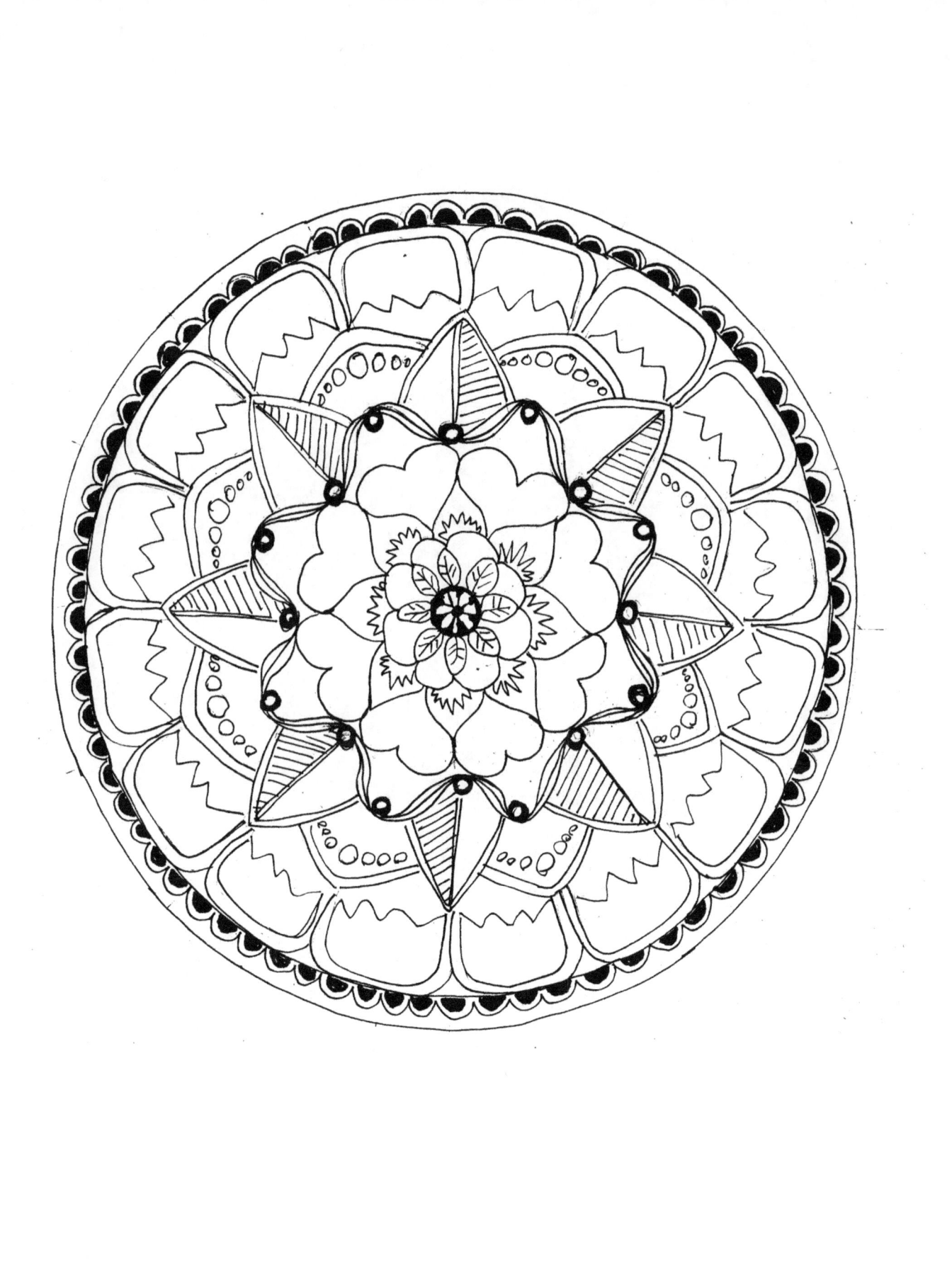

THE AMAZING WORLD OF GROWNUP COLORING BOOKS

In today's fast moving world everyone need something to help with stress and anxiety. One thing that is becoming very popular is adult or as we call them Grown-up Coloring books.

We design and publish coloring books for adults and children. As our introductory offer, we are offering a one year subscription for our coloring books. One year subscription will give you 2 coloring books per month for 12 months or 24 coloring books.. That is a saving of $165.00 or more over the retail price of adult coloring books per year.

Order today and receive box of colored pencils to get you started.

Adult coloring books are becoming very popular. They help with stress and anxiety management, ADHD and epilepsy patients also benefit by coloring. Coloring is fast coming into it own. More and more people are buying Adult coloring books. Same as kids coloring books but with more detail.

We are introducing a new subscription to our coloring books. For $75.00 per year you can receive 2 coloring books per month a total of 24 coloring books . This is an awesome savings of $165.00 per year or more for coloring books. You will also receive 12 colored pencils to help getting you started. Tell two other people about our coloring books and if they buy our subscription we will send you a set of colored pencils with 100 count. That is 100 different colors to choose from when you are coloring. TO order your subscription please fill out the information below. Be sure to include $75.00 cash check or money order for fast processing. Mail to: The Artist Korner , 190 county rd 41, Heflin, AL 36264 Customer Service. 1(256) 201 7584

Name:_____

Address:_____

City:_____St:_____Zip:_____

Phone:_____

Email:_____

Referral:_____BJ1011_____

| For Office use Only |
| Received: |
| Date: |
| Shipped |

Order your books today and receive 2 books each month. Plus 152 count box of color crayons, Refer two friends who become customers and we will send you a box of colored pencils 100 count.

TO order: please fill out the information below. Be sure to include $75.00 cash check or money order for fast processing. Mail to: The Artist Korner , 190 county rd 41, Heflin, AL 36264

And you thought Coloring books were only for KIDS. Benefits of Coloring Books for Adults

Coloring is fast coming into it own. More and more people are buying coloring books because coloring is not just an activity for keeping kids occupied anymore. People are finding out how coloring can benefit their lives and health. Coloring is no longer only a child's activity. In reality, coloring books and coloring pages for adults are also extremely therapeutic and can help generate well-ness, and peace of mind. Coloring eliminates negative thoughts. It relieves stress and anxiety. It is no wonder that, coloring books for adults are so popular these days. When an adult colors these patterns, He/she actually experiences mindfulness and even reaches a meditative state. This has even been proven by several scientific studies. With so many therapeutic benefits of coloring pages for adults, it is time that every adult learns the benefits of coloring.

Coloring pages for adults help relieve stress.

I have been carrying my art with me to the doc office for years. It has helped me tremendously with anxiety attacks. When asked why I brought my art work to the appointment. I told them it was my Prozac and I didn't need any pills. It helps a person to be-come calmer and experience less stress and anxiety.

HOW COLORING EFFECT US

When we pick up a color for a particular shape or pattern, we activate the analytical part of the brain. On the other hand, when we choose to mix and match colors, we activate the creative side of the brain. This helps incorporate both areas of the cerebral cortex which control vision and help with coordination and fine motor skills.

Coloring prevents Negative and damaging thoughts

When an adult colors, he or she is pre-occupied with what they are doing and prevents most negative thinking to take place. Color-ing helps with Stress, anxiety, ADHD and much, more.

Drawing is like Prozac only not a pill.

Meditation is the art of doing nothing. It is also the art of not concentrating which helps relax and reduce the chatter of a restless mind. While most people find it difficult to meditate, coloring pages and books for adults easily help induce the same meditative state. Coloring relaxes the mind and makes a person more mindful. It also keeps him/her focused on the present moment-just like meditation!

Color you anxiety away

Anxiety is a common mental condition affecting hundreds of adults. Anxiety and panic attacks cause many symptoms including: thoughts of death or dying, excessive worry, nausea, headaches, chills, fever, insomnia, etc. By using coloring pages for adults, therapists help their adult patients relax. The artistic expression helps patients go deeper into a relaxed state making other forms of therapy more effective. Research has now proven that coloring pages and books for adults can be used as prelude to regular or conventional therapy for many mental disorders. I didn't color the books I drew them and published them. But it has the same effect. Drawing and coloring. It depends on who you are and your abilities.

Coloring for adults helps them re-discover themselves

Adults often find themselves stuck in a rut managing jobs, housework etc. Coloring pages can help one get out of this routine, mak-ing them feel more comfortable and relaxed at the end of a long day. This activity can also help one be with his/her thoughts. Many an adult has rediscovered him/herself through coloring pages for adults online and offline and relax with this wonderful ac-tivity at the end of a long day.

Coloring for adults is a perfect therapy many diseases

Coloring books for adults are ideal for patients -especially those battling health issues like epilepsy. It easily calms a person down and relaxes them which, in turn, help alleviate epileptic attacks. No matter what the health problem, coloring gets your mind off of it and helps you relax. You recover faster

Coloring for adults helps spark creativity

One of the most important benefits of coloring books for adults is that they help ignite creativity and keeps the mind active.   This is why it may be beneficial for those who have dementia and Alzheimer's. Coloring books and pages also help people become more creative in their lives.

Coloring books for adults help transport one to a time and place faraway.

If, at the end of the day, you really wish to relax and get away from it all-simply bring out your crayons and start coloring. This will surely help you get out and away from it all and help you relax and unwind. It is like taking a vacation without going anywhere!

GET Free Stuff, Discounts and News.

Earn Bonus Points when you Purchase new books.

Earn points when you refer someone who purchases books.

Earn Points when you send us a testimonial about our books.

Also receive Discount coupons, Rebates so join our newsletter list and receive mailings and emails News about new books and discounts and sales. You will also receive pointers on using colored pencils and crayons water colors and other mediums.

Name:_____

Mailing address:_____

City:_____State:_____Zip:_____

Phone:_____

Email:_____

Receive a 10% Discount certificate when you join our mailing list. Receive another 10% discount coupon when you send us your testimonial about the books you have purchased. These coupons may be used together to purchase your next book. Plus earn points towards another purchase. Of coloring supplies.

www.ingramcontent.com/pod-product-compliance
Lightning Source LLC
Chambersburg PA
CBHW080258180526
45167CB00006B/2583